Bellingham, WA 98225
jacksarajane@comcast.net
autobiography 31,481 words

WITHOUT APOLOGY: A FAMILY CHRONICLE (Book I)

by JACK DUKES

ISBN 1452831718   EAN-13 9781452831718

JOE AND ZINA

This chronology begins with a genealogical dead end. It is not always a pretty story. The facts and rumors of our heritage (your heritage) that I saw or knew of are all here. In cases where my memory has failed, I have used directed imagination, i.e., I know the way they spoke, what they ate, what they smelled like, their education (or lack of it). I feel confident that my fill-ins are accurate. There is a box full of documentations of every kind for any of you that choose to continue this chronicle.

By this book, you will know your beginnings. You will learn of the incredible hardships my parents and maternal grandparents had to go through so that you could be born. Do not think for a second that you would be alive if any of them had failed in their life's missions.

My father, Joseph William Dukes, was born on July 30, 1910 to a prostitute mother. She had no idea who the father was. Joe was the product of a rape.

Joe's mother, Mabel, nee Dukes, gave Joe her own father's name. When he was but eleven, she threw him out of her house and onto the streets of San Antonio, Texas. Her new boyfriend didn't like kids and, to Mabel, getting rid of Joe was an easy release from the terrors of single motherhood in 1921 Texas.

Joe hawked newspapers, pulled weeds, washed windows and slept wherever he could, mostly along the banks of the San Antonio River. His experiences there forced him into a hard-working, self-reliant, do-whatever-it-takes adulthood.

Jess and Rose Heiner (I and my two sisters, Jeannine Jo and Donna Carol, were required to call them "aunt" and "uncle" and say "yes, sir" and "no, ma'am" had befriended Joe and took him into their hearts but not their home. I have no idea of what the reason was. However, they stayed friends and visited each other a lot. Aunt Rose died in the forties and Jess just disappeared. I remember her most for her gift to me of a bright red bicycle she bought for five dollars. It was barely a bicycle, just a frame and two wheels, but I totally loved it for the freedom it gave me.

Joe attended a one-room school for a while but he was too far behind to catch up so he never finished the 6th grade. He was 19 before he saved enough money to buy a second-hand Indian Motorcycle. Why he ever came to Muscotah, Kansas, no one ever knew. Grandpa said it was because he got a girl in the family way and her brothers were after him. If that is true, then we have unknown and unknowable relatives in Texas. Joe wouldn't talk about it.

The largest building in town served as grocery store, gas station, tavern, and town hall. Located on Kickapoo Street, it was also a snack bar specializing in hard-boiled eggs and pickled pigs' feet. It was Joll's favorite place to hang out. He wasn't there on the day that Joe rode into town on his roaring motorcycle. He shut it off beside the porch, got off and stood beside it.

"God, it's hot!" said Joe to the farmers sitting in the shade of the porch. "Any cold beer in there?" Prohibition was still in force, but everywhere you looked, there was a mini-brewer, a wine maker, or a gin specialist.

"One or two," said the only non-overalled man sitting there as he arose and held open the screen door. "Go, ahead, kid. I reckon you own that there bike. You sure couldn't steal anything that loud!"

"Hell, I ain't no thief. Lord knows I've been desperate, but not that desperate. Know any place I might get a day's work around here?"

"As a matter-of-fact, I do. Joll Smith is a laid-up Spanish-American War veteran. He got shot and it flares up on him once in a while. He can't do nothing heavy then. His old lady's a wheelchair-confined cripple. He's got a couple of teenaged kids. They try hard, but they can't do it all. He's only a sharecropper but if he don't produce, he don't get a share. He can't pay you anything, but you'll get a place to sleep and some pretty good grub. Sarah's a real good cook. Interested?"

"Sure am! I ain't had me no home cooking in quite awhile!"

"Ok. Take the north road out of here; keep going until you see an old, weather-beaten clap-board home and that's it."

They took their beers back out onto the porch and sat guzzling and gossiping until Joe finally left with his noisy muffler. He finally saw the isolated farmhouse from a high spot in the road. It sat on cleared land in the midst of four cornfields. Joe drove up the long, long driveway, past the substantial vegetable garden, past the cherry and apple trees, one on each side of the driveway, with a giant old live oak close to the house and almost as tall as the second-story window. Joe rode up the pathway as slowly as he could to keep the muffler noise down. All four of them: Joll Rupert Smith (52), his wife, Sarah Belle or Bell (37), in her wheelchair, Zina Ellen (16) and Carroll William (14) were gathered on the front porch, side-by-side, watching the stranger chugging and snorting his way to the porch. He sat his bike on its stand and waited.

"How do?" asked Joll (my grandfather). "What can we do for you?"

"Howdy," said Joe (my father). I'm Joe Dukes. I just learned that you could maybe use a hand around here."

"Is the law after you?" asked Joll.

"Nope. I'm an honest man."

"Can't pay you nothing. I can only wait until the harvest and give you part of my share."

"Suits me. You got a place for me to sleep?"

"In the barn. There's a cot in a small room there."

"What about chow?"

"You hungry? Zina, fix him up with something to eat and drink and bring it out here. It's too hot to be inside. Black coffee okay? I like it strong."

Joe nodded. "Much obliged," he said.

"We'll share our table with you. This is Sarah, my wife. You can see she's crippled up but she can sure cook! That was Zina and this is Carroll. Don't ever call him Carl. He hates it. And keep your hands off of Zina. I catch you fooling around, I'll kill you." The serious look on his face was suddenly replaced with a hearty laugh. "Welcome, Joe! Tell us something about yourself."

"Hell, there ain't nothing to tell about me. I'm a Texan. I ain't got no family. Nobody cares if I'm dead or alive. I'm hard-working and I'm honest. And that's all I'm gonna say. The rest of it, you'll see for yourself." Zina brought out a plate of chicken and baked beans. Joe wolfed the food down without wasting a second. Sarah smiled at his appreciation.

"You're going to be easy to cook for, Mr. Dukes. I'll see you don't go hungry."

"Thank you kindly, ma'am. I wonder if you could show me where I can bed down and take care of my bike. I'm pure-D tired."

"Carroll, you show him but don't dilly-dally. He needs his rest."

"I'll do it! I'll do it!" said Zina as she jumped off the steps next to the bike. "I ain't never seen a motorcycle before." She turned to Joe. "Can I ride it? Is it safe?"

"Maybe tomorrow, if it's ok by your folks. Good night."

Joe lay down on the half-twin bed and went immediately to sleep. Zina lingered, stroking the motorcycle all over, until Sarah called her.

It threatened to rain on that first night that Joe spent in the barn. The thunder awoke him about 2 or 3 AM. He heard wind whipping through the other side of the barn. He checked to ensure his motorcycle was safe. It was, and he went back to sleep immediately.

The rooster began crowing just before the sun rose. Joe awoke like an animal. His every sense was immediately alert. It was a trait that he would keep for the rest of his life. He sniffed the air and smelled only the ripe aroma of the barn. In a few seconds, he relaxed and started to remember his greeting and luck in finding a job. He grinned and danced a little circle while he shoved his clenched fists in the air. Just then, Zina came out.

"Howdy," she said. "I came out to collect the eggs. Wanta help me?"

"Shore. How many eggs you get?"

"About a dozen, I guess. Why?"

"I reckon I could eat a dozen all by myself."

As they chatted, she moved closer to the henhouse. He followed. "Mom's making flapjacks this morning…with sugar syrup and fresh-churned butter."

"Girl, you're killing me!"

"Aw, you. She's doing it for you, you know," she said and giggled.

"Are you as accommodating as your ma'?"

"Whatta you mean by that crack? You ain't gettin' fresh with me, are you?"

"Forget it. I didn't say a word."

"Ok. You comin' in?"

"Gotta wash up first."

"Trough's on the other side of the barn. More privacy that way. Hurry up." Zina trotted off with her egg basket and checked behind once to see if he was watching. He was.

You can pretty much guess what happened next: Zina and Joe fell in lust. But Zina, my mother, held out for a ring. She got one. On September 1st 1929, they were married. I was conceived around the 9th of December and born on August 9, 1930. Zina was 17.

JACK

On August 9, 1930, a scream funneled out of the upstairs window of the old isolated farmhouse. Zina's mother, Sarah, in her wheelchair, waited downstairs hoping to hear a newborn cry. The only sound she heard was her husband, Joll, and Joe in the kitchen.

"Don't worry, Joe," said Joll. "There's a jug of tomato wine in the ice pit. You want some?"

"Sure."

The ice pit was under the house and lined with bales of hay. The dank smell of the bottom layer overpowered the onions, potatoes, and other edibles stored in bins formed by the bales. Joll extracted a jug labeled, "TOMATO". He blew out the lamp as he climbed to the outside of the two-story, weather-beaten house.

Inside, he sat the jug on the kitchen table and went to the cupboard to fetch two tumblers. "This oughtta make you feel better."

"Thanks, Dad. Wonder what's taking so blasted long?"

"She's new. Lots of heifers have trouble with their first born."

"Wish I had your calm about it."

"Wait'll you have a couple. Then you will."

They heard another scream. Joe sat his glass down and turned pale. "What's wrong?"

"Ain't nothing wrong, Joe. It's coming, that's all."

Joll pushed the tumbler towards him. Joe picked it up and drank it down like water. Sarah disapproved immediately.

"Shame on you men! You especially, Joe. Your wife's in hard labor and you're sitting here guzzling it down."

"Well, what the hell can I do, Ma?"

"Somebody downstairs, bring me some more towels and hot water!" hollered the doctor.

"Do what he says," said Sarah. "You know where the towels are."

Joe got up, took a teakettle from the stove and ran upstairs with it. Sarah wheeled over to the linen closet and took out every towel.

"Where the hell's the towels?" growled the doctor.

Joe, without answering, ran downstairs, grabbed the towels from Sarah and ran back up again. "How's she doing, Doc?"

"Just fine. The head is just starting to move. Should be over with soon."

"Anything else I can do?"

"Not now. Leave me be."When Joe was halfway down the stairs, Zina screamed again. Joe froze momentarily, and then rushed the rest of the way to the kitchen table. Joll had already poured another glass. Joe drank half of it down.

"Slow down, son. No use in getting drunk."

Another scream interrupted Joe's reply. He finished off his glass and shoved it over for more. "Goddamn. Why's it have to hurt like that? You think she's putting on?"

"No, she ain't putting on!" said Sarah angrily. "The Bible says we shall be in travail at childbirth. You think about what you did to make her this way, then you can hang your head in shame."

"A husband's got rights!" snapped Joe, also angry.

Joll laughed. "You got the right to feed and clothe your family, that's all. I ain't touched Sarah in a coon's age."

"You ain't never gonna touch me again either, Mr. Smith," said Sarah.

This time, Joll drained his glass.

"Joe, come up here!" yelled the doctor. "Bring a lamp."

Joe complied. He was there for over ten minutes. When he returned, his face was ashen and he was trembling.

"What's wrong, Joe?" asked Sarah.

"The baby's not coming. It's stuck. She's too small for it. The doctor said it's because she's underdeveloped. My God, what am I gonna do?"

"Sit down and take it easy," said Joll.

"You don't understand!" yelled Joe. "The doctor told me to decide which one I wanted saved, my wife or my baby."

"Dear Jesus," said Sarah. "What did you tell him?"

"I told him if I can't have both, I don't want neither."

"You bastard!" yelled Sarah. "You've killed my girl! Take me upstairs, both of you."

Sarah lifted her body onto a chair. Joll moved first and bumped up the stairs with the wheelchair. He returned and clasped hands with Joe to make a seat for Sarah. They moved up the stairs until she was back in her wheelchair.

"Get away now. Leave me be. Go back to your boozing."

Joll and Joe left reluctantly. There was no quarter in Sarah's voice or eyes.

"What's wrong, doctor?" she asked.

"She's too young. There's not enough pelvis. The baby's head is through, but its shoulders won't come."

"What are you going to do?"

"Use forceps. It may kill the baby, perhaps Zina, too, but it's the only chance I have to save both of them."

"If you have to, doctor, forget the baby. Save my daughter."

"That choice isn't yours, Sarah. Her husband has already made it. Zina doesn't belong to you anymore, she belongs to Joe."

Sarah wheeled to the head of the bed and took her daughter's hand. Zina was wet with sweat and tears and groaning softly. She had stuffed a towel in her mouth.

"Do what you have to do, doctor," said Sarah in a flat voice.

The doctor inserted the forceps and manipulated them until the baby's head and neck was firmly in its grasp. Then he started to pull. Zina screamed, the sound muffled by the towel.

"Come on, come on, come on," pleaded the doctor as he placed his foot on the end of the bed for more leverage. Finally, the child, bleeding from the forceps, came out. Zina fainted. Sarah cried. The doctor cleared the air passages, but no breath was taken. Slap. Slap again. No sound.

"Joe!" he hollered.

Joe bounded up the steps, Joll close behind.

"Get me some ice and fresh water. Joll, empty out this basin."

"What is it, Doc?" asked Joe.

"It's dead," said the doctor. "Do what I said. It's my only chance to save him."

Joe started to speak again. Sarah interrupted him. "Run! Damn you! Run!"

Joe rushed to the ice pit and retrieved a twenty-pound chunk. He dumped it into a copper wash tub. "Ice pick," he demanded. "Where the hell's the goddamned ice pick?"

"Take it easy. You'll get more done and better, too."

"YOU take it easy!" exploded Joe. "That's MY baby up there."

Joe found the ice pick and savagely drove it into the chunk. "Don't ruin the washtub," cautioned Joll. "I'm going up with the water. Come on."

The doctor laid the baby on the bed, poured steaming water into one basin and ice into the other. When they were full enough, he dunked the baby into the ice water, then into the near-scalding water. The baby gasped for breath, then began crying.

The doctor, tears streaming down his face, wrapped it in a towel, handed it to Sarah and attended to Zina. "You have a son, Joe."

Joe reached for the baby. Sarah held it away from him. "You gave him up, Joe. My daughter, too. I ain't never gonna let you forget that."

Joe looked to Joll for an ally. Joll just turned his palms up and shrugged.

"Ma," said Zina, "is the baby all right?"

"Just fine, honey, you can take him now."

Sarah looked again at Joe, her face a frozen commitment. "Never."

The next year was spent in caring for their ample vegetable garden. Grandma canned what we didn't eat. She sold the canned items all year long. It was the only source of steady income our two families had. The two men occasionally got jobs, mostly dealing with the damage the dust bowl had created. The soft, powder-fine dust got into everywhere. The use of water quickly turned it into mud. Dad and Grandpa liked working with each other. It was as close to fun as they could get. Grandma always got the money, less the beer money. Grandpa always held back on his money. Grandma had learned to ignore it. She needed flour, salt, and thread. Not much more. She used the flour sacks, (which were prettily designed just for that), to make all of her own dresses and Mom's, and my diapers. They used the scraps for their menstrual days. And so the days progressed, wearily the same. Then one morning, without preliminaries, Mom announced her pregnancy.

MOVING ON

Zina!" screamed her mother. "What the hell you mean you're pregnant again! The doctor already told you not to have any more kids. I'm going to poison that son-of-a-bitch husband of yours. I'll feed him some death mushrooms! Don't he know you're anemic? Or don't he care?"

"Ma, I don't care. I know I'm not going to live long anyway and I want all the kids I can have."

"Well we can't go on living here then. You know what you and your stupid husband have done? You screwed us out of house and home. I hope you're proud of yourself."

"I am. At least I'm honoring the first commandment, "Be fruitful and multiply." She giggled.

"Don't you get smart with me. I don't know what the hell we're going to do."

On a Sunday afternoon, everyone was on the porch, enjoying the peace and quiet, when a car appeared on the road in. Grandpa knew the car.

"Welcome, Mr. Whaley! I hope!" Grandpa's baritone voice boomed out with confidence despite the obvious sad conditions that afflicted all green stuff around, except their garden but including the corn acreage he was responsible for.

"'Fraid not, Smitty. I got nothin' but bad news. First is, you ain't gonna get no share this year. I know you and your family worked hard but this goddamned dust bowl has beat us all. You were lucky to have your vegetable garden." He got out of the practically new Ford, too new to even have its paint faded. He stepped up onto the porch and shook Grandpa's hand.

Grandpa said, "Well, we pumped a lot of water every day for 'em. Wish we could have done the same with the corn."

"Well, that ain't all. After payin' off the money I lent you after the last crop's failure, you still owe me $150.00."

"Whaley, you know I'm good for it. We had a little misfortune this year, never mind the drought. I got a bullet so near to my heart that they can't take it out. That's how come I get a veteran's pension. Got it with Teddy's Roughriders in Cuba. Not like when I formanned a Mex working gang on the railroad."

"I know, and I also know you got another mouth to feed. And a wife who's crippled. And a daughter who can't do much and a son too young to be of much good. I wish I could help you, Smitty, as God is my witness. The best I can do is forgive you the $150.00 you owe me if you move out by the end of this month. I got a healthy Negro couple to do what you can't. Don't take it personal. It's just business. So long, Smitty."

As soon as the sound of his car began fading, Grandma wheeled her way to the door. "What was that all about?" she asked.

"We gotta get out of here by the end of the month. There's hell to pay and no water hot."

Dad joined Grandma. "What's wrong, Ma?"

"Got any money, Joe?" asked Grandpa.

"Under two bucks."

"Well all I got is a hard-on. Can't sell that anywhere or we'd be rich." His laugh was almost a cackle but it was infectious. The others began grinning, except for Mom.

"Daddy, don't talk like that. I expect to see you completely break your cussing habits before Jackie starts to talk. You too, Joe." Her shock of bright red hair glistened as she turned to address both men. "I mean it!"

"We got anything we can sell, Ma? Maybe some Cherokee thing or something?" asked Grandpa.

"No, but I got some money. The Bible says we gotta tithe, but God hasn't been too good to us in recent years. So, I've been putting 10% of every dime that crosses my hands in an old stocking. It's under my mattress. Go get it, Joe."

Dad took off as Grandpa came inside. "You been holding out money from me?" he asked in anger.

"So what if I was? You'd just spend it on your wine-making stuff. At least I got it when it counts."

Dad came back with an opaque stocking. "Dump it on the floor and let's count it. Zina, you're good at counting. Why don't you total it up?"

Mom began stacking the coins. Then she counted the nine one-dollar bills. "You got $21.19."

"Joe, you're gonna have to sell your motorcycle" said Grandpa.

"Like hell I will!" exploded Dad. "You ain't got no right to tell me what to do!"

"Sure, I do" said Grandpa. "If it weren't for me and Ma, your son and wife would both be dead. You owe us, not the other way around."

Dad's anger was still on his face. He loved his bike. Mom broke in. "Honey, Dad's right. And we don't need it no more. How you gonna carry me and two babies? Ain't no way."

"Tell you what," said Grandpa, "let's me and you go down to the Kickapoo Tavern and hear what the old boys have to say. Ma, give me four of those dollars. We'll have to buy a round or two."

Grandma, having been through this too many times, handed over the four bucks with a sigh and no words. At this crisis in their lives, she didn't want to get Grandpa mad. His temper was explosive and knew no limits. He was always ready to fight with knuckles, knives, or guns. He enjoyed telling about killing two Mexican gang workers who planned to waylay him after he gave one of them a beating. He laid the Mexican over a water barrel and whipped his bare ass with a knotted, wet rope while others held him down.

One of Grandpa's more civilized gifts was a facility with languages. He spoke fluent Mexican and overheard their plans. He was ready with his six-shooter when he deliberately walked into the ambush. With two shots, both of them were dead. No one cared. It was just the way things got done.

The next day, Dad and Grandpa boarded the cycle and took off.

"Dad," said my dad, "be careful to keep your feet away from the muffler. It'd melt your toenails."

"Ok, son, goose her and let's get gone." Dad drove respectfully, not wanting to get Grandpa upset.

The men on the porch were just gathering, all carrying coffee mugs. Even though all but one was dressed in overalls and flannel shirts, they didn't look alike. Fat, slim, short, tall, different postures; it was easy to tell them apart. They stood shoulder-to-shoulder, watching the approaching noise. Dad shut the cycle off. At once, the men said, "Howdy, Smitty! Howdy, Joe. Ain't seen you in a coon's age, Smitty. Whatcha been up to?"

"Just trying to stay alive. Ain't got nothing but shank's mares you know. Can I buy you boys a round? I got something pretty serious to talk about."

"Smitty, I hope you boys don't take this too personal, but we'd like you and Joe to step off the porch. Don't you folks ever bathe?"

"Why shore we bathe. Every Saturday night. Trouble is the cisterns are dry and we only got the one hand pump. The babies are the only ones that get bathed every day. Sure didn't mean to offend you."

After getting the beers and saluting Grandpa, they all listened quietly until they heard the whole story. George, the corn-crib manager spoke first. "I'm glad to hear it! You oughten to not be working a nigger's job. Go to St. Joe. I hear the packing plants are gonna be hiring soon. Some government deal. It'd be a damn sight better for all concerned."

"Ain't got no way of getting there, George. What brung us here in the first place is rusting out in the cornfield somewhere. Joe, here, is willing to sell his motorcycle but it ain't gonna be nearly enough."

"Tell you what," said George, "I've got an old beat-up Dodge dump truck out back. I'll trade you even; even give you a fill-up. But you gotta teach me how to ride it. I'll teach you how to advance and retard the spark, choke it, and crank it without getting your arm broke. Deal?"

"Deal!" said Grandpa as Dad frowned but kept his mouth shut. Grandpa beamed as he shook George's hand.

After their tediously long trip, punctuated by two flat tires, rest stops in the weeds and the two babies constantly squalling, they reached St. Joseph on its south side, famous for its nonstop stockyard smells. After their final mile, they left the highway (Route 66) on Myrtle Street. The first thing they saw was a saloon at the apex of the two streets leading away. There was a sign in the window: "House for Rent".

"Let's go check it out," said Grandpa. They pulled up and parked the dump truck on the wrong side of the street. There was no traffic. Dad went in with Grandpa. Grandpa had gotten another dollar from Grandma.

"Two beers," he ordered as they bellied up to the bar. "Tell us about this place you've got for rent."

"Well, it ain't got nothin' but an outhouse. Needs cleanin' out. No water 'cept for the yard pump in the well. Got a hand pump in the kitchen. Got a wood kitchen stove, three bedrooms, no bath. Cistern leaks but I could fix that up…assumin' we get some rain. Ten dollars a month, payable in advance."

"Two more beers," said Grandpa as he walked out to the truck. "Gimme ten dollars," he said to Grandma. She handed it over without a word.

Grandpa returned to the saloon, took the "for rent" sign out of the window, carried it to the bar, slapped it on the counter with the ten dollars and said, "I reckon you might welcome us home with two on the house."

The barkeep, fat, friendly, and flocked in a white apron, grinned and said, "How about some wine instead? Homemade. Out of turnips."

"The hell you say," said Grandpa. "I've made tomato and dandelion wine but I ain't never heard of turnip wine."

The barkeep poured three glasses. Grandpa drank before Dad. Dad was holding back, slightly intimidated by the prospect of turnip wine.

"Hot damn!" said Grandpa. "Now that's good drinkin' wine. Would you be kind enough to oblige me by givin' me the particulars?"

"Shore. Glad to do it. After you all get settled in, I'll bring over a jug for your welcome home party." He laughed heartily in his slightly tenor voice. "Welcome, by God! Welcome! My name's Greek but just call me Bud."

Moving in was no big deal. A few pots and pans, clothes, and tools, and the job was done. We all slept on the floor: the women and babies lying on blankets; the men on the bare floor. The men woke up with hangovers; the women with excitement.

Dad opened the door in answer to Bud's knock. "Hi, Bud! Welcome to our new home!"

"I see you folks ain't got too much furniture. Tell you what. The last people who lived here got behind on their rent. One day, they just hauled ass outta here in the dead of the night. I took their furniture and stored it in a back room at the saloon. You folks want it you can have it for $50 cash or $75 in payments."

"Well, I'd like to see it first," said Grandma.

"Go right ahead. You gotta take it all though. I need the room."

Dad, Grandpa, and Grandma left Mom behind to watch us babies. The furniture had been well cared for. Grandma liked it at first sight.

"We'll pick it up right after breakfast," said Grandma.

"Well, now, maybe you'd like to fix it over here. Whip up a bunch of scrambled eggs for us all. I got a customer who pays me half-'n-half with eggs."

"I'd surely be glad to," said Grandma, "and thank you for your kindness."

Breakfast was spent getting to know about each other.

"Know anywhere we can get work?" asked Grandpa.

"Not really. You any good with animals?"

"I know a thing or two," said Grandpa.

"One of my customers has a pig farm. He ain't got no money but he's got a small herd needs castrating. He'll give you a slaughter pig if you can help him."

"I'll do it," said Grandpa, grinning. "I always wanted to de-nut something."

"Oh, Joll," rebuked Grandma. "Mind your manners."

"I'll set it up," said Bud. "Your backyard is boarded in. I reckon you could slaughter it there."

Dad and Grandpa had a hard morning at the farm. They had to round up and corral twenty-one pigs. After corralling, the pigs had to leave, one-at-a-time, by a slip chute that trapped them but left their scrotums exposed. Dad herded the pigs; Grandpa sat on a milk stool so he could grab the scrotums. He sliced open the scrotum, popped out the testicles, and cut their attachment cords with a tool that looked like a large pair of pliers. One edge of them was super sharp, the other edge a corrugated crushing surface. With one movement, the testicles were detached and the cords crushed. It took less than ten seconds each pig. Of course, handling the herd was time consuming as were the frequent stops for talking that kept tensions from building too high. When they were done castrating, they had a pail of forty-two testicles. They would be sold as delicacies.

"Damn!" said the farmer, "you sure work good together! I 'preciate that. I'd be pleased to call on you again should the need arise. Take a pair of them pig balls home with you. No charge. Come on. I'll show you your sow. She ain't breeding true so I can't afford to feed her. Damn fine job boys. Much obliged."

The pig was docile all the way to their backyard, which was surrounded by a six-foot closed fence with one ten-foot gate. No neighbors' prying eyes to fear here. Grandpa brought out his 20-gauge, single shot, Sears & Roebuck shotgun. He climbed into the truck and killed the sow with a single shot to the space where the head is joined to the neck. The pig fell without a sound. Leaving it to bleed out, they all went into the tavern to enjoy some well-earned beer.

Grandma said to Bud, "I saw the pile of wood ashes by the back gate. You gonna use them?"

"Naw. If you can use them, they're yours."

"Much obliged. Between the hog fat and the ashes, I can brew up a mighty fine soap."

"It's a good idea. I can help sell your overage."

"Mighty fine of you, sir. I do a lot of canning in-season. Perhaps you can help me sell some of that."

It seems now to have been an actual out-of-body experience, as was the peeing story. In each case, I floated above the action and can see it yet today. It is a genetic truth, we are smart people. We are also psychic. Grandma's vision of the death of her son (coming later) did not come from her Christianity; it came from our (your) Indianhood. I am 15% Cherokee as per a DNA test. The rest of me is Indo-European. I feel that the psychic part of our heritage exists even within a drop of gene-pool stuff. It is basal and primal.

A final memory of this stage of our lives: Mom and Dad were fighting for possession of a paring knife. She was trying to take it away from him while he threatened to "kill that goddamned brother of yours." They stopped yelling at each other briefly, just long enough to give me a dime and a bucket to get some more beer at the next door saloon. I numbly did as I was told and took the bucket (almost as tall as I was) into the deserted saloon. The owner told me, "No, it's against the law." Befuddled. I just stood there, holding the bucket. Mom and Dad both came for me. They loved me up a lot but that did not cleanse me of my fears

LOYALTY

Everybody had their own jobs to do. My job was to take care of. Jeannine. I always had to take care of Jeannine, ever since she was two and I was three. Lots of times I didn't like it, but, later on it was fun. We learned to kind of stick together against the grownups.

One good thing about moving was the dump truck the new landlord gave us to save having to haul it away. Dad and Uncle Carroll worked on it until they got it running. Jeannine and I would watch them put the crooked handle into the front of the motor and crank it until it ran by itself. We learned a lot of good words that way. We couldn't say them in front of the grownups, but we said them to each other.

Our new home wasn't very pretty, but Grandma liked it a lot. The land it was on was shaped like a piece of pie. A saloon was at the tip, Mabel's Place, then us, then a big warehouse, so we had no neighbors. The men liked it because they could get a bucket of beer for a dime right next door. Grandma like it because she could make lye soap and render lard from the pigs Dad and Uncle Carroll brought home when they'd help out a farmer. I liked it because the backyard was full of weeds as high as my head. I had a piece of broomstick I'd hit against a weed so hard it would fall over. It made me feel strong.

One day, Jeannine and I were playing in the backyard. She had of bunch of tin cans she was stacking up. I had my broomstick. There was a big pile of wood ash by the back fence that Grandma used to make lye soap. I was seeing how high I could make the ashes go when I hit them. Then I thought I'd play a trick on Jeannine.

"Whatcha buildin'?"

"Nothin'."

"Whyn'tcha see how big you can stack 'em? Then I'll knock 'em down."

"If you do, I'll tell on you."

"Baby. Tattle-tale baby."

She didn't say no more. She just stacked them up as high as she could like she was daring me. So, I did it. I swung the broomstick as hard as I could right at the middle of her stack. She stuck out her hand to protect them and I hit it right square on. She started bleeding and crying at the same time and ran into the house.

I knew it was her own fault for sticking her hand out like that but the grownups wouldn't think so. The stick had some blood on it, so I threw it away right into the thickest weeds. Instead of disappearing, it laid on top right in plain sight. If Momma came outside, she'd see it right away and take it away from me. She only stuck her head out the back door though.

"Jackie, you get in here this instant!"

"I didn't aim to, Mommy. She stuck her hand in the way."

"Get on in here!"

When I went in, Grandma was looking at the finger. The tip of it was almost torn off right from where it bends. It was hanging by a little piece of meat and skin.

"Seems to me we ought to cut it the rest of the way off," said Grandma.

"Momma," said my mother, "we can't do that. She's just a little girl."

"Well, the only other thing we can do is try to sew it back on. Fetch me my sewin' basket."

When Momma came back with it, Grandma took a small curved needle and purified it in a match flame. Then she started sewing with the smallest thread she had. Jeannine stopped crying and started screaming. Every time she yelled, I felt worse and worse. I started believing it really was my fault. Every time the needle went in and was pulled through, my own finger started hurting. Pretty soon, I was crying too. They didn't pay any attention to me, though. They were too busy with Jeannine. When they were done, Jeanine was just crying again.

"Don't cry, honey," Grandma said to her. "Indians don't cry. Be a brave girl."

When I heard that, I shut up crying. I wanted to be like a brave Indian. Grandma was awful proud that her mother was a full-blooded Cherokee daughter of a chief.

"Oh, Mom, let her cry. She's just a little girl, you know. We ought to sterilize the cut."

"Fetch me Joll's whiskey bottle, then." When she went to do it, Grandma finally looked at me. Her look made me wish I was somewhere else. "I swear, we can't leave you kids alone for two minutes. What in the world did you do, Jackie?"

"It weren't his fault, Grandma. I stuck my hand in his way."

Mom was coming back. "Wasn't," she said. "You just saved your brother a lickin' when Daddy gets home."

I looked at Jeannine. She had a worried look on her face.

"Thanks," I whispered and smiled. She kind of smiled back but still hurt too much to do it right.

"Jeannine, this is gonna hurt some but it's the only way to kill those nasty germs. Try not to cry," said Grandma. She poured some whiskey into a shot glass and held Jeannine's finger in it. She screamed and tried to pull away but Grandma held her tight until her finger was good and soaked. Then she took a clean, white towel, cut off a strip and wrapped it around the cut.

"There," she said, "it's gonna be good as new."

"You tell your sister how sorry you are," Mom said to me.

That wasn't hard so I did it right away.

"I'm sorry. I didn't aim to." Then I took her and gave her a big hug and kiss. Mom and Grandma both smiled and I knew they weren't mad any more.

"You go outside and play," said Mom. "Your sister's gonna lay down for a while."

I went out and got my broomstick back. Then I took into those weeds like it was their fault. I kept it up until my arms were too tired to do it anymore.

One day I had a chance to make even with Jeannine. We didn't have a coal stove, only a kitchen stove that burned wood. When the men went hunting or fishing in the old dump truck, they'd bring back a load of wood. Daddy and Uncle Carroll would saw it but leave the splitting to when they needed it. Jeannine decided to split some. We'd both watched the men put a piece on the chopping block and hit it with a single-bitted ax. It looked easy but the ax was longer than Jeannine and almost too heavy for her to lift. As soon as I saw her trying it, I tried to take over.

"Gimme that ax."

"It's my ax. I had it first."

"No, it's not. I'm the oldest and I'm the boy. You have to do what I say. Girls don't split wood."

"I can too."

I grabbed the handle in the middle. The end was almost touching the ground. The blunt end of the blade was towards her face, the sharp end towards mine.

"You gimme it," I said.

"You let go," she said.

Instead, she let go. The blade caught me right in the middle of the forehead, just above my eyebrows. There was a lot of blood, but it didn't hurt much. I decided to teach her a lesson, so I fell down and acted more hurt than I was. I groaned.

"I'm sorry! I didn't aim to."

I moaned.

"Get up. Come on, get up."

Silence.

"You get up or I'll go tell Mommy!"

Collapse into total limpness.

"Are you dyin'?" She shook me. "Jack, please don't die!" She started crying and I felt ashamed of myself. I got up and hugged her, getting her all bloody too.

"Don't cry. I was only foolin'."

"You scared me."

"I did?" I couldn't help giggling. I was so proud of myself for fooling her. "Guess I was a pretty good actor, huh?"

"You sure was. Please don't ever die."

"I won't. But you gotta promise not to cry, neither."

"I won't."

Hand-in-hand, we walked back to the house to get the hurt treated. There was blood all over my overalls and her flour-sack dress. Mom screamed when she saw us. Her face turned as red as her hair.

"Which one of you's hurt?" she asked.

"I am but it don't hurt none."

Grandma looked at us with that hard look that meant she was mad as could be. She shook her head so hard her black braids wiggled all the way down to the ends. "Get me some more towels, Zina," she said to Mom. "You kids take off them clothes right now."

Mom started pumping water out of the pump at the sink. "How'd it happen, Jackie?" Mom asked.

"The ax slipped and hit my head. I was gonna split some wood."

"Well, you leave that ax alone from now on. You're too little."

I looked at Jeannine. She was smiling a thank you. I smiled back at her. "See?" I whispered. Now we were even.

SARAH BELL, 1935

"Grandma, can I ask you a question?"

"What, Jackie?"

"Grandma, how come you have to use crutches?"

Her dark eyes tightened, then closed. "Well," she said, "if you're old enough to ask, you're old enough to know. God punished me for something, and to this day, I don't know what for. It came to pass that I needed an operation. Something was wrong inside my belly. Well, they gave me a shot in the spine, low down. The needle slipped, or the doctor didn't know what he was doing, or God guided his hand. Anyway, the shot paralyzed me from the waist down. I was bedfast with two wonderful children to care for.

"I was bedfast for a long time…years. Grandpa was good to me back then. He was good to the kids too, your mother and Uncle Carroll. Then one day, he started to get mean to me. He'd come into my bedroom where I lay helpless and start yelling at me. He said horrible things about my not being a real wife, mother, or even a woman. And he wouldn't stop. Finally, it was every single day, morning and night. I just couldn't take it anymore.

"One day, I hauled myself out of my bed with just my arms while he and the kids were away. Then I crawled to the kitchen, my whole lower body just dragging behind. I was gonna fix his supper, but I couldn't. I couldn't reach anything. So I just laid there and cried.

"He came home and found me there. I thought he was gonna yell at me some more, but he didn't. He just stood there, looking at me, not saying a word. I was ashamed to look up at him. The mess I'd made in my clothes only proved his point. I wasn't a woman anymore.

"He stood there quiet for so long that I finally had to look up at him. He was crying without making a sound. I never saw him cry before or since. He was still crying when he helped me back to bed.

"I didn't understand it at first. It took the longest time for it to sink in that he was right. I wasn't a woman anymore. I wasn't a real woman. I was only a bedfast cripple. Right then and there I decided that I wasn't gonna lay in bed until I died.

"To this day, he won't tell me how he got the money to do it, but he hired a doctor to come out to the farmhouse. Hour after hour, day after day, the doctor pushed and pulled and twisted and shoved my back and legs. Pain like you wouldn't believe.

"Do you know about pain, Jackie? I don't think so. You know what hurt is when you stub your toe or get spanked, but real pain is different. Real pain doesn't just happen to your body, it happens to your mind too. I pray to God you never have to go through it.

"Anyway, Grandpa stopped yelling at me. The kids started telling me I would walk again. I started half believing it. Oh, Jesus, forgive my unbelief!

"Finally, I was able to use crutches and a wheelchair. The more I did it, the easier it got. I needed help in bathing and Grandpa was glad to do that. He kept wanting to touch me on my privates. I wouldn't allow that. I thought that maybe that was what God was punishing me for.

"Then one day, I had a vision. I saw my own dear mother, a full-blooded Cherokee and daughter of a chief. I was wide-awake when it happened. She didn't say anything to me. She just kind of floated there in mid-air, but I sensed what she was trying to tell me. She was saying to turn my back on the white man's ways and go back to the Indian ways. So I did. Then, with the Depression and all, Grandpa had no job. With no money coming it, we picked poke greens and paw-paws and mushrooms and berries and black walnuts and wild honey. I rendered my own lard from hogs Grandpa got for working on farms. I made my own soap using our woodstove ashes. And lots and lots of stuff more. When you're a little bigger, you'll learn to do all those things and hunt too. I'll bet you'll be a great hunter."

Just then, a knock on the screen door made it rattle.

"It's me, Miz Smith. Julie. Miz Smith, Sadie's in some real fierce pain. She wants you to come right away so's you can pray for her."

"Oh, dear Jesus. Jackie, get your shirt on. You have to come with me."

I caught the tone of her voice and moved fast to obey. She rolled her chair over to the corner where her crutches were and heaved her big body up on them.

"Hurry up, Jackie."

I held the screen door open for her and watched her slug her way down the three porch steps. She walked by throwing one leg ahead at a time, then moving her crutches one at a time. It was a slow pace, giving me plenty of time to look around.

Grandma's house always looked out of place. It looked ugly when you compared it to the houses around it. They were all clean and mostly white. They had picket fences covered in whitewash and green lawns that were always mowed. We had nothing but hard-packed dirt where a few dandelions grew.

Between the curb and sidewalk, there were lots of trees. They were oak and elm and cottonwood and some more I didn't know the names of. They made the sidewalk a lot cooler. When we left our own neighborhood, in about five blocks, the poor peoples' houses started. They always made me glad I didn't live there. There were no more trees or lawns or fences, just hedges that were never trimmed. Their front lawns were hard ground, just like ours. Sadie's home looked the worst of the lot.

We heard Sadie screaming two houses away. It seemed she didn't hardly stop to take a breath. Grandma started to walk a little faster but I lagged behind. I was afraid of all that pain. When we reached the porch, Grandma put both crutches under one arm and waited for me to catch up. By now, I could hear the words inside the screams.

"Jesus, dear God, take me! Oh, please, please let me die!"

"You stay here, Jackie. Wait on the porch. Sadie, I'm here. I'm here, Sadie." I listened to Grandma start praying. "Oh, please, dear Jesus, have mercy on this poor soul. End her suffering and take her into your loving arms."

The prayers did no good. The screams continued. I looked through the screen. There was an awful stench, like rotting garbage, only worse. I saw Sadie lying on her back. I watched her scream and beat the air with her fists. I watched Grandma sitting on a chair at the edge of the bed, hands first together in prayer, then touching her friend like she was trying to make the pain go away. Grandma prayed as much as Sadie screamed. She finally stopped praying.

"Sadie, I have to go now. The girls will be coming home soon and it ain't right for Jackie to be hearing all of this. Try to get some rest, dear."

"Oh, God! Don't leave me Sarah!"

"I have to, dear. Zina's bringing the girls over."

Sadie's little release from the pain finally ceased. She began screaming again and her prayers changed. "Oh, Satan! Please help me, Satan! Take me to your bosom and let me die. God doesn't care. Take me, Satan!"

Grandma leaned forward from her chair beside the bed and slapped Sadie hard in the face. "Shut up!" she yelled. "Oh, God, I pray for your forgiveness from this blasphemy. Forgive her for she knows not what she says."

"Forgive me, Lord," prayed Sadie. "Forgive me and end my torment. Take me, please, take me."

Grandma, crying, heaved to her crutches and left, promising to come back as soon as possible. She joined me on the front porch. I kept quiet on the way back home, wondering what to say.

"Grandma, what's wrong with Aunt Sadie?"

"She's got cancer, honey, real bad. It's so bad the pain killers don't work anymore. Poor soul. Her whole belly's being eaten up inside."

"Why doesn't God help her?"

"I don't know, Jackie. I just don't know."

I was quiet for a little bit, then I said, "I hate God."

"Jackie, don't talk like that! It's a sin."

"I don't care. God lets too many bad things happen. I hate God."

I began to cry. Grandma looked at me quick-like, and then she started to cry too. We walked side-by-side all the way back to our own neighborhood before we stopped crying.

CHRISTMAS, 1939

Billy and I were best friends. Indeed, I was the only friend Billy had. My dad worked for the WPA, the Works Project Administration, fathered by President Roosevelt to boost the USA out of the Great Depression. Billy's dad didn't work at all. He was an alcoholic jailbird. Billy was glad to see him go to jail. The beatings stopped then.

I looked forward to Christmas. My wish list included a bike, a BB gun, and a pocketknife. I knew I would get one of them. I dreamed I would get all three. Billy expected nothing. Religion, especially Christianity, was not tolerated in his tar-paper shack of a home. Neither was "Toys for Needy Children". Billy's dad said, "If'n I cain't give 'im nothin', then nobody's gonna give 'im nothin'." I knew this. I told Billy, "If'n I get 'em, you can ride my bike and shoot my BB gun and whittle with my knife."

Christmas grew near and my dad got laid off. My mother got sick at the same time. My dad gave me the bad news. "Son, don't expect much for Christmas. Your mom's gonna be in the hospital and I just ain't got no money."

Billy gave me some good news. His dad had been arrested in drunken brawl in a barroom. He would be gone for ninety days. I told him of my own father's job loss and no Christmas presents forthcoming. I was almost crying.

"Don't cry, Jack. We got each other, you know." Billy put his arm around my shoulder and I didn't cry.

I had a special relationship with my grandmother. She was old, poor, half-Indian, and lived her life in a wheelchair.

"Be there a reason why you boys can't make something for each other?" she asked when I came to her in despair.

The lights came on for me. I could hardly wait to tell Billy. Billy's lights came on too. "Let's keep it a secret," he said. "Let's really surprise each other."

Christmas came. I got fruits and hard candy, socks and underwear. Billy got nothing. That afternoon, Billy and I met under the scoreboard in the snow-covered baseball field. Each of us had a small package. Mine was wrapped in the Sunday comics section; Billy's was in a brown paper bag.

"Hi Jack! Merry Christmas!"
"Hi Billy! Merry Christmas to you too!"

We held onto our gifts, not quite knowing how to present them. Billy finally held his out and said, "Here."

"Thanks, Billy. Here's yours."

I opened mine first. It was a rubber band shooter made out of wood. It shot bands cut from inner tubes. "Just what I always wanted!" I said. "How did you know? Open yours, quick!"

Billy tore the paper off, opened the box inside and yelled, "Thank you! Thank you!" In the box was a forked branch t rimmed into a Y-shaped slingshot. "I love you, Jack!"

"I love you too, Billy. Think we could go down to Stink Crick and shoot some frogs?"

"We gotta ask our folks first."

"Ok. Hurry up. I'll meet you there."

It started snowing again while we were at the creek. Huge flakes came down from a windless sky and coated us with purity. The water ran a sluggish black between the white-coated banks. There were no frogs, of course, but we didn't care. We had each other.

ZINA

"Did you get it?" asked Grandpa.

"Sure did," said Dad. "We can move in this weekend."

"Thank Jesus," said Grandma. "I don't want to seem inhospitable, but your three kids are a little much for a woman in a wheelchair."

"I know, Mom," said Mom. "I really appreciate being able to stay with you and Dad until Joe got his feet under him. Thank God for WPA!"

"It ain't much," said Dad. "It's kinda ramshackle and rickety. The landlord said he can't paint it until we've been there awhile. Says we have to build up some rent equity, whatever that is."

The four of them sat around an oilcloth-covered kitchen table that sat on torn and worn-down linoleum. Unlike the Kansas farmhouse, this house, at 411 Kentucky St., had electricity. A single bulb hung from the ceiling directly above the table.

"There's something else too," said Dad. "This place has a flush toilet. It's out in the barn and the tenants in the other half use it too, but it beats your outhouse."

"Quit braggin'," said Grandpa. "I have to carry Sarah's slop jar out every day. Want some dandelion wine? Seems you got a reason to celebrate."

"I'd be obliged," said Dad.

."You know how you argue over religion. It's enough to make a body sick when you do that."

"Don't worry, Ma," said Dad. "Besides, we got something else to celebrate."

"What's that?" asked Grandma.

"I'm pregnant again, Ma," said Mom. "It's been two months now."

"That ain't nothin' to celebrate," said Grandma sharply. "Joe, you know the doctor said no more kids when they took out Zina's spleen for leukemia. You think that makes you some kind of man? Ridin' her to death like that? You're killin' my baby." She turned to Zina. "And you're alettin' him do it. You ain't got the sense God gave a goose."

"Now, calm down, Sarah," said Grandpa. "There ain't no harm been done yet. No sense in hollerin' before you're hurt. Let the kids be."

"That's a fine way for you to talk. You gave me two kids but there's no tellin' how many little bastards you got runnin' around."

"Yeah and with damn good reason too. I'll get that wine out of the cellar." He left.

The three of them sat nervously, not knowing what to say next. Mom broke the spell.

"Have the kids been good today?"

"Good as you could expect. Donna whines about bein' afraid a rat's gonna bite her in the ass every time she has to go to the outhouse. Jeannine ain't much better. She sure has a smart mouth for a seven-year-old. Jackie's the only one I can count on. At least he helps keep his sisters in line."

"I'm sorry, Ma. I know it's been hard on you."

"Not nearly as hard as it's gonna be on you."

Grandpa came back with an earthen jug labeled "Dandyline". He got two water tumblers from the cupboard and filled them to the brim.

"Here's to you, Joe. You sure know what to do with a woman."

"Oh, Dad," protested Mom.

"You drink your stomachs rotten if you want to. I'm going to bed," said Grandma. "I'm going to say a special prayer to our Lord Jesus tonight. I can't tell what I'm going to say, but don't be surprised if your ears burn and that goes for all three of you. Good night." She wheeled off to the room she refused to share with Grandpa.

"You want some wine, honey?" asked Grandpa.

"No thanks, Dad. I think I'll go to bed too. Joe, what are we going to do for furniture?"

"Don't you worry about that," said Grandpa. "There's enough old stuff up in the attic to get you started."

"Thanks, Dad!" said Dad. "I was kinda hopin' you'd help out."

"Joe," said Grandpa, "did you know there's a place in the Bible that says they ate their own dung and drank their own piss?"

"Dad!" protested Mom. "You should be ashamed. Good night you two. Joe, don't be long."

"I won't honey. Good night."

I was playing in the rubbage that half-filled the old barn where the bathroom stool was. I made trucks out of boxes and castles out of cast-offs and had a lot of fun.

"Zoom! Crash!" I said as my truck smashed down a castle. In the wreckage, I spied a sardine can.

"Oh, boy! There's a boat!" I said out loud to myself. I promptly began sailing it in the stool, looking around first to make sure no one could see me.

"Zoom! Bang!" I sailed my tin can back and forth in the water of the stool. I stuck my hand in and created waves that made the boat sink. Rapt in the constant banging and sinking and starting over again, Mother's voice barely got through to my ears.

"Jackie! Jackie, come on in and eat!"

Once the message got through, I felt guilty and fearful right away. Surely Mother would somehow know what I'd been doing. She would tell Dad and Dad would get mad. I pushed the boat down into the stool and pulled the flush chain. Away it went. No trace was left of my forbidden treasure.

"Comin' Mommy! I just had to go to the bathroom."

The toilet did not stop up immediately. Liquid passed through until solid material finished the blocking that the tin ship started. When Dad came home from his WPA job, Mom gave him the bad news. Dad and the neighbor's son, who had been sentenced to CCC work to avoid the reformatory, tackled the task of unplugging. They fastened a tin can to a long, stiff wire. They dipped the smelly stuff out into a bucket. Finally, they came to the sardine can. Dad became furious. There was no doubt at all in his mind that I put it there. After the reflushing and clean-up was done, he stormed into the house.

"Where's Jack?" he yelled at Mom. Mom was in the kitchen, the room closest to the barn.

"He's in the front room. What's the matter?"

"He plugged up the toilet, that's what's the matter. I've told him a hundred times if I've told him once not to put anything into the toilet. Now, by God, he's going to pay for it."

"Joe, you're not going to hurt him. He's just a little boy. He didn't do it on purpose."

"Purpose or not, he disobeyed my rule. If you don't like to see him spanked, you can leave."

"Joe, no, please."

Dad shoved past her and went into the front room, grabbing her hairbrush on the way. "Jack!" he shouted. "Why'd you plug up the toilet? Here I try to make things decent for us, and all you can do is mess them up."

"I didn't, Daddy."

"Don't you lie to me!" he shouted even more loudly. "If there's one thing I won't stand for, it's lying!" He grabbed me by the arm and jerked me forward. Thwack! The hairbrush landed on my rear end. I immediately began to cry. It only made Dad madder. Thwack! "You quit your squallin'. I haven't even begun to teach you a lesson!" Thwack! "Why did you do it?"

I twisted away from him to run to my mom. She was running to meet me. We met in the middle room where the potbellied coal stove glowed cherry red. Dad chased after, jerked me away from her and started hitting me over and over, hollering for the truth, demanding that I confess and be sorry. Mom finally managed to get between him and me. Their upper bodies met in a struggle for the hairbrush. They looked like an upside down V. Both were screaming at each other. Mom finally won and, though she had no replacement nor hope of one, threw the hairbrush into the stove. Dad stormed out, angry and muttering. Mom turned her attention to comforting me.

Seven months later, Mom was in the hospital again, trying to deliver her fourth child. It was the same hospital where they had removed her spleen in a fight against leukemia. It was a Sunday afternoon. Dad was getting the three of us ready for a visit to her.

"What's Mommy in the hospital for, Daddy?"

"So she can bring you a new brother or sister."

"I don't want another sister," I frowned. "I want a brother to play with."

Dad laughed. "That's up to God, son. We have to take whatever He gives us."

Dad finished putting my clothes on me. At eight-years-old, I was washed and polished into a state rare for me, even to go to Sunday school. "You go outside and wait for me to get your sisters ready. Stay clean or you'll get a whippin'."

"All right, Daddy." I went outside, feeling virtuous in my cleanliness. As I walked around the grassless yard, the boy across the street, Mike, saw me and came over to visit.

"You goin' somewhere?" he asked.

"I'm going to see my mother. She's in the hospital."

"You sure are clean."

"I know it. I have to stay clean until we get back or I'll get a spankin'."

"Where'd you get them nice clothes?"

"Grandma made them for me. She made some for my sisters too."

"What'd she make them out of?"

"I dunno. Some old clothes, I guess."

"You mean they ain't new?"

"Of course not. We can't afford new."

"They look too clean to me. Let's get 'em dirty." Mike, 13, and a head taller than me, picked up a clod of dirt and threw it, hitting me on the thigh. The clod left a dirty mark.

"Quit it!"

"Quit it yourself," said Mike and threw another clod. I tried to brush the dirt off.

"Here, let me help," said Mike and began brushing my clothes. Trouble was, he had another clod hidden in his hand. It left new marks all over.

"Quit it!" I yelled and pushed him. Mike, face screwed up in ugliness, pushed back. I fell down but got up again at once.

"Quit it!" I yelled again, loud enough for Dad to hear and come to the window. He stayed silent as he watched me get pushed down again.

"Say uncle," demanded Mike.

"I won't," I said, but this time I was slow in getting up.

"Jack," said Dad sharply, "you whip him or I'll whip you."

That's all I needed. With both arms swinging, I tore into him. Mike, surprised by the attack, merely defended himself at first. Then, using his superior height and weight, he grabbed my head in a hammerlock and began beating on my skull with his other fist.

"Give up! Give up!" he said. "Say uncle!"

"Don't you dare quit!" yelled Dad. "Don't you ever quit!"

I managed to tangle my legs into Mike's legs and we both tumbled to the ground. Mike landed on his back with me on top of him. His wind was driven out of his body and the hammerlock was broken. I placed my knees on his shoulders and began hitting him in the face. One blow got him right in the nose and took all the fight out of him.

"Uncle! Uncle!" said Mike but I kept right on hitting.

Mike, with a hard effort, threw me off and got to his feet. His open palms were extended towards me in a gesture of surrender. Now filled with a rage that took over control of my mind, I ignored it. With both arms swinging, I tore into Mike again. My small fists tattooed all over his face. It was more than Mike could take, more than he could defend himself against. He began crying and tried to run away. I chased him all the way back across the street to his own yard. I stood there, trembling, while Mike let himself into the house.

"That's fine, son. Come on back now," hollered Dad.

I returned to my dad, now out in the yard.

"I'm proud of you, son," he said as he brushed the dirt off my clothes. "I don't ever want you to start a fight, but I never want you to run away from one. You stay here until I finish with your sisters. You look alright."

I was proud. On the bus on the way to the hospital, I bragged to my sisters. "You should've seen him run! I just hit him and hit him and hit him."

"Didn't he hit you back?" asked Jeannine.

"He sure did! He tried to make me say uncle but Dad told me never to give up and I didn't. I was just like a windmill. Boy, he better never try that again!"

"Are you going to tell Mommy?" asked Donna.

"I sure am!"

"How could you beat up on a bigger boy? Weren't you afraid?"

"I was more afraid of Dad. He said he'd whip me if I didn't whip Mike."

"Ok, you kids. This is where we get off. Remember now, I don't want any squabblin' between you in the hospital. Son, you're in charge. Can you handle it?"

"I can handle just about anything."

"Good," he smiled. "You'll have to wait in the waitin' room until the doctor says it's ok. Let's go."

He left us kids and went off to Mom's room. He was only gone for ten minutes or so. When he returned, he was fighting back tears. We knew at once what was wrong, although we had no words for it.

"Come here, you kids. Daddy's got some bad news. Your mommy isn't comin' back."

"Not ever?" I asked.

"Not ever," said Dad. "She's gone to Heaven. So has your little brother."

"Aw gee whiz," I said. "I really wanted a brother."

"So did I," said Dad, "and your mother did, too. Let's get out of here. I'm takin' you to Grandma's house."

"Don't we even get to see her?" complained Jeannine, starting to sniffle.

"No," said Dad. "Let's get out of here."

We were quiet on the way back from the hospital. Dad made us wait on the front porch while he went in to talk to Grandma. It wasn't until we heard her scream that we started to cry. I put my arms around my two sisters.

"Don't worry," I cried, "I'll take care of you. I'll take care of both of you. I'll never quit."

Dad and I were sitting on the bank of the Missouri River, waiting to run our bank lines. Dad had been to the stockyards, where he worked off and on as an animal driver, and picked up two cull chickens. When we got to the river, he wrung their necks, cut 'em open and used their guts for bait.

He set out fifteen bank lines, each one of them a three-foot willow branch with about four feet of line. He knew we'd catch mostly carp, but he was hoping for a catfish.

"Do I have another Grandma or Grandpa?" I asked him.

"Well, son, you do, but I ain't got no idea where they might be. Hell, I don't even know if they're alive. My momma, your other Grandma, well, she weren't a very good woman. She told me once she didn't even know who my daddy was."

Dad stopped and stared at the brown water swishing by. I kept quiet, afraid to break in on him, fearful that he would shut up and say no more about it. When he spoke again, his voice had changed from a serious mood to one of happiness.

"Hell, boy, my ma didn't get married until I was eleven years old. Her old man and I didn't get along so she kicked me out of the house. I've been on my own ever since. I sold newspapers on the streets of San Antone for grub money. I took care of myself pretty good…for a boy. I learned to fish and trap and sleep out in the open. I almost never had to beg.

"One time when I did, this old man and old lady took me into their house. I stayed with them for about a year, then I run away. They was always on me about school. Hell, I knew how to read and write, but that history stuff and shit like that, I just couldn't cotton to it. By the way, how you doin' in school?"

"Alright, I guess. The teachers make me sit up at the front of the class 'cause I can see the blackboard better. I don't like it though. I always think everyone's awatchin' me. It makes me nervous."

"Well, I want you to get a good schoolin', better than I got. I figger if I can get you off to a better start than I had, and you can get yours off to a better start than you got, well, hell, we just naturally got to succeed. Let's go run them bank lines. Oughtta be somethin' on 'em by now."

Dad picked up the bucket with the chicken guts in it and started down the bank, me right behind. The first line we came to had a carp on it.

"Run back and get me that gunnysack, Jackie."

I obeyed and held the sack open while Dad dropped the fish into it.

"Think you can carry it?"

"Sure, Dad."

"Well, like I was sayin', Aunt Rose and Uncle Jess were the finest people I ever met until I met Sarah and Joll. Them two's good enough so's you don't need any more grandparents. There ain't nothin' in the world I wouldn't do for them. They think the world of all you kids...whether you deserve it or not. You know that?"

"Yes, sir. Grandma likes me best."

"Yeah, I know. She pisses me off sometimes the way she caters to you. You ain't gettin' a swelled head over it, are you?"

"No, sir. Sometimes I wish she'd be more fair. I don't like it when Jeannine and Donna get left out."

"I don't like it neither. Still and all, her heart's in the right place." By now, he'd checked and rebaited six more lines. "It's a poor day for fishin'. Water's too high. All that rain washed too much feed into the water. Wait a minute! Would you look at that?"

I saw, two poles down, a huge swirl of water left by a very big fish.

"God damn! We got us a big cat!" said Dad.

"God damn! We sure do!" I answered.

He stopped briefly. "When we get home, you get your mouth washed out with lye soap. You gotta learn how to keep a civilized tongue in your head. Bring that gunnysack." He pulled the fish out of the water. "A ten pound flathead if it weighs an ounce! We'll eat good tonight. Here, take a look."

He held the fish up in front of me high enough so that its tail was even with my face. The fish suddenly flopped, hitting me in the face. I promptly peed my pants. When Dad realized what had happened, he roared with laughter. Me, red-faced again, said nothing.

"By God, that's the funniest thing I ever did see! Well, come on, boy. Take 'em off and rinse 'em in the river. Reckon you'll have to go home wet. Hurry up now."

He ran the rest of the bank lines while I rinsed my pants.

"Let's go home, boy. We'll leave the lines out overnight. God damn! I can hardly wait! Have I ever got a story to tell! Let's go home."

TEDDY

I ran half-a-block ahead of Dad and my two sisters to get to Grandma's house first. I slammed open the screen and rushed in at full speed.

"Hi Grandma! Hi Grandpa! Where's Teddy?"

Teddy came flying out of the kitchen into the front room, purple tongue out half-a-foot, teeth bared in a dog grin and ran smack into me, almost knocking me off my feet. He broke my hug around his neck and knelt before me on his forelegs. He wanted to play.

"If you wanna romp with Teddy, you go out in the yard," said Grandma.

"Come on, Teddy!" I said and both of us raced through the house and out the back door.

"Those two sure do make a pair," said Grandpa to Dad as he came through the door.

"Hi, Joll. Hi, Sarah. You two all set to go berry pickin'?"

"Soon as Paul gets here with the pickup," said Grandpa. "You stayin' here with Jack?"

"Sure. Can't take the dog along and Jack wouldn't go without him. Besides, it'll be good for us to have some time alone. He's nine now and needs to learn some man stuff."

Teddy was a big dog. He had his father's short hair and his mother's red color and purple tongue. He loved to rear up, plant his forefeet on peoples' shoulders and lick them in the face. He did that one time to the neighbor lady in the corner house. She was unmarried but pregnant. Nobody in the neighborhood liked her. To get even, she looked for every opportunity she could to be mean. She called the police, then came and told me about it.

I put Teddy on the back porch with its slanted floor where all the seldom-used household items were stored. Then I went through the house and locked every door that could be locked, including the closet doors. I went out on the front porch and waited in the porch swing. When the police came, all I could see was the big guns on their hips.

"You got a dog here named Teddy, son?"

I was afraid to trust my voice so I merely shook my head no.

"This is 411 Kentucky Street, ain't it? The Smith's house?"

I nodded yes and felt the silent tears start down my cheeks.

"We got a report that your dog attacked a woman on the street. Where is he?"

By this time, Grandma arrived at the front screen in her wooden wheelchair. "Hello officers. Teddy didn't attack no one. He's just playful, that's all. The woman who turned him in, she's just a little hysterical, that's all. Poor soul's got a right to be, I reckon, seein' as how she's pregnant and all and doesn't have a father for the child."

I managed to speak my worst fear. The words came with tears, though without sobbing. "You ain't gonna shoot him, are you?"

The older policeman took pity. "Naw, we ain't gonna shoot him. He your dog?"

"No, sir. He's Grandma's but he likes me best."

"Well, you're gonna hafta keep him tied up. Can't have him jumpin' around on pregnant women. No tellin' what might happen."

I felt my face flush with relief. I was still a little scared though, so I shut up and let Grandma do the rest of the talking.

"We got a clothesline in the backyard. We can put him on that and then he'll be able to run back and forth. He's a big dog and needs his exercise. Would that satisfy you?"

"Whatever you do is ok with us, Mrs. Smith. Just don't let him get out on the streets again."

"We won't, officers. I promise."

"Good day to you ma'am."

No sooner had the police gone than my tears got the best of me. I opened the screen and crawled, sobbing, into Grandma's lap.

"There, there. Teddy's safe now. I got a shoulder harness left from his mother. You wanna put it on him?"

"Ok."

That night, when Granma told the story, no one seemed to mind about the incident. Instead, everyone laughed at how I had locked all the doors, including the closet doors. Red-faced at first, I finally joined in the laughter.

"How'd you get that black eye?" Dad asked me.
"A kid at school."
"You give him one too?"
"No, sir, he was bigger than me."
"Who started it?"
"He did. He was makin' fun of the patches on my pants."
"He hit you first?"
I hesitated before answering. "No, sir," I said in a low tone.
"What'd I tell you about startin' a fight?"
"Not to."

"Well, hell. Ain't you ever gonna listen to what I tell you?"

"No, sir...I mean, yes, sir." "You need a lesson on how to protect yourself. Go get them boxin' gloves you got for Christmas."

Dad stayed in the kitchen while I reluctantly obeyed. We were the only ones in the house, the rest of them having gone berry picking. The kitchen cupboards were painted a dull green, Grandma's favorite color. The wooden drop-leaf table had a red-and-white oilcloth on it. Teddy lay under it, nose on forepaws, watching every movement in the room just by rolling his eyes.

I knew what was coming. I'd had these "lessons" before. Dad always managed to hit me hard enough to make me cry, then pretended he was sorry. When I returned, Dad put out his Bull Durham cigarette in the Mason jar-lid ashtray.

"Put 'em on," he said.

They were too small for him. All he could get in were his fingers.

"Stand up here now and put up your guard."

I did and Dad thumped me hard on top of the head.

"You gotta bob and weave. You can't just stand there. No wonder you got a black eye." He knelt in front of me. "Now we're nearer the same size. Let's see if you can hit me."

I half-heartedly made a pass at his chin. He deflected it.

"You gotta do better than that. Go ahead, try real hard to hit me in the face. I won't spank you."

A minor rage suddenly took over my mind. I flurried into him with both gloves and actually landed a blow on his nose that brought tears to his eyes. He reacted at once with a slap that made me cry. At the same time as he rose to his feet, Teddy came out from beneath the table. He planted both forepaws on Dad's shoulders and snarled and growled right in his face. Dad's face turned white. He backed away until Teddy was back on all fours.

"Jesus Christ!" he said. "That damn dog...that damn dog...Jesus Christ!"

My tears stopped at once. I grabbed Teddy around the neck and hugged him. "Good dog, Teddy!" I whispered in the dog's ear. I looked at Dad. "Can we stop now?"

"Hell, yes! I ain't never gonna try to teach you nothin' about boxin' until that damned dog's not around. You better put him out on the clothesline."

I held out my wrists for the gloves to be untied and taken off. Then I took Teddy out of the back door. Once alone, I hugged Teddy again.

"Good dog, Teddy! I wish you could be with me all the time." I stayed outside with him until Dad called me back in.

Teddy got loose one more time. He picked the same neighbor lady to jump up on. This time, the police were not as nice.

"Get rid of the dog or we'll have to have him destroyed."

The neighbors across the way and two houses down were movin' to a farm in Kansas. They agreed to take Teddy. Though heartsick about it, I tried to be brave.

"You'll have a good home, Teddy. Grandma and Grandpa both say so. You can run on the farm and be free. You won't never have to worry about police or nothin'."

Then, crying, I went to my room where I cried myself to sleep. The next day, when I got home from school, Teddy was gone. Three weeks later, he was back. Grandma, hearing a scratching at the door, opened it, and Teddy, paws bloody from a four-hundred-mile journey through unknown territory, jumped into her lap and fell asleep.

For one brief moment, I thought he was back for good. Grandma told me different. "He's gotta go back to the farm, Jackie. I'm sorry."

I shut myself in my room, refusing to see Teddy again, until, two days later, Teddy was reclaimed. I overheard his new owners.

"We'll keep him tied up until he gets used to the new place, Mrs. Smith. Don't worry. We like him a lot. He'll have a good home."

"Jesus Christ," I prayed that night, "why'd you hafta take Teddy away? First my momma, then Teddy. I ain't never gonna love anything again."

CRIME

"Hi Bobby!"

The reaction was instantaneous. My friend's face turned red, the tendons in his neck stood out, and his hands turned into fists.

"You call me Bobby again and I'll knock your block off. Bobby's a girl's name. My name is Bob."

"Ok, ok, sorry. I didn't mean nothin'. I came over to play, not to fight."

"Well, ok, then, but you better not do it again."

"I won't. I promise. What shall we do today?"

"Let's go steal something," he said.

I had ridden my bike over to Bob's house for a Saturday of fun. It was early on a bright, warm morning.

"Ok. What shall we steal?"

"I dunno. Just stuff."

"Let's go to Harmon's Grocery. They got lots of stuff to steal." We got on my bike and rode off.

"You go in first," said Bob when we got to the store.

"No, you."

"Let's go together.

"Ok."

It was too early in the morning for the store to have customers. The clerks were busy stocking shelves. Bob and I wandered about unchallenged. When we walked down the aisle where the Kool-Aid display was, I nudged Bob and pointed with my eyes. He nodded yes. A split second later, we were on our way out with a package of Kool-Aid apiece. I had lime; Bob had grape.

We both got back on the bike and rode to the baseball field where we hid beneath the billboard. We tore open the tops of the packages, wet our fingers, dipped them in the Kool-Aid and licked them clean. We each ate about half the contents before growing tired of it.

"You ever smoke?" asked Bob?

"Naw. My Grandpa gave me some chewin' tobacco once. It was awful."

"Me, neither," said Bob. "You want to?"

"Sure. You got some?"

"No, but I know where we can steal some."

"Where?"

"The Corner Tap. All we gotta do is for one of us to keep the bartender busy while the other one cops the cigarettes."

"How we gonna do that?"

"He keeps his cigarettes at the front of the bar. One of us has to get him to the back of the store."

"How?" I asked.

"Here," said Bob as he handed me a tube of lipstick.

"What am I gonna do with this?"

"You go back to use the bathroom, then scribble something on the wall. Come out and tell him about it like someone else did it. When he goes to see, I'll hook the cigarettes and some matches."

"Great idea!" I said. "You gonna be a crook when you grow up?"

"Naw. I'm gonna be a teacher. This is just for fun."

The plan worked perfectly. By the time the bartender had checked, Bob was out the door with a carton of Marvels and a book of matches.

"Where'll we go to smoke 'em?" I asked. "Back to the ball field?"

"Naw. I know of a better place—the haunted house."

"What haunted house?"

"It's on Becker Street. No one lives in it. There's supposed to be a woman's leg in the attic and a milk bottle full of brains in the kitchen."

"Wow!" I said. "Let's go!"

We gained entry through the back door where a missing pane of glass allowed us to reach through to turn the lock. I left my bike out by the alley. Once inside, we roamed the whole house. I had never been inside such a grand one. It was obvious that others had used it. There was trash strewn about with little piles of it in the corners. Whiskey and wine bottles dotted the refuse. We couldn't find our way up to the attic but we saw the bottle of brains in the kitchen.

"Goll!" I said. "Look at that! They look like real brains!"

"How do you know what real brains look like?" challenged Bob.

"My uncle likes to eat sheep brains scrambled with eggs. Dad and Grandpa eat 'em too. Grandma can't stand 'em. She makes the men cook their own."

"How do you suppose these got here?"

"I dunno. Maybe a killer uses this place...a mad killer."

"Shut up," shuddered Bob. "Let's go smoke."

We went onto the back porch to smoke and discuss what we had seen. We each ripped open a pack and cautiously tried to light them.

"You gotta suck in on it," said Bob.

Soon, we had our cigarettes going and couldn't figure out what all the attraction of it was.

"Let's try two at a time," I said. We did. Then three. Then five—the most our lips could hold. It was still unsatisfactory.

"We oughtta inhale," said Bob.

"You first."

"No, you."

"Let's do it together."

"Ok."

Bob cheated. I inhaled and promptly choked until I vomited. Then we went on another exploration. Both of us were jumping from the stairs, trying to reach the prisms of the chandelier. They were just out of reach. That's what we were doing when the cops came in.

It was too late to hide. I was more afraid than Bob. Not of the cops, but of the leather thongs hanging from their billy clubs. I expected a beating. Instead, we were put in the back of the squad car and taken to headquarters.

All of a sudden, I remembered the half pack of Kool-Aid in my pocket. The rear window of the squad car was open about an inch. I cautiously slipped it out and through the opening. My feeling of relief was short-lived as we reached the station.

"We didn't do nothin'," both of us told the police captain.

My house had no phone so Bob's mother was the only one notified. She came to pick him up. I was driven back to my bike.

"Ridin' double, huh?" said one of the cops.

"No, sir, we was takin' turns."

"You go straight home now. We'll be comin' over later to talk to your grandma."

"Yes, sir."

No matter how slowly I pedaled, my house grew inevitably closer. I dropped my bike in the front yard and went in, a picture of despair.

"What's wrong, Jack?" asked Grandma.

"Nothin'. The cops are gonna come."

"What on earth for?"

"They'll tell you. I'm goin' to my room." And I did, staying there until the police left and Grandma called me out.

"You're grounded for a whole month," she said. "No bike, no play, no goin' outside. You understand?"

"Yes, ma'am."

Within a week, she relented. I went straight to Bob's house. It was another beautiful Saturday morning, but Bob wasn't out in the yard. I went to the door and knocked. Bob came in answer.

"Jack! What are you doin' here?"

"I came to play. Come on out."

"I can't. I'm grounded. Besides, Mommy and Daddy are mad at you. I'm not supposed to play with you anymore."

"Mad at me? Why me?"

"Daddy had to pay a hundred dollars."

"A hundred dollars! Gee whiz!"

"He says it was all your fault."

"My fault! It was your idea!"

"Bob, who are you talking to?" yelled his mother from the kitchen.

"No one, Mom," he yelled back. "Jack, you better go."

"Wait a minute. It wasn't all my fault."

"Yes, it was."

"Is that what you told your folks?"

"Why not? It's the truth."

"Gee whiz, Bob, I never thought you was a rat."

"Bob," said his mother as she came into the living room, "who…Jack! How dare you show your face around here. You leave Bob alone. He's never to play with you again."

"But, Mrs. Hanson…"

"You hear me, Jack? You get on away from us. You are not welcome here anymore. You're white trash, that's what you are. You get on out of here."

"Boy, Bobby! You wait 'til school starts! I'm gonna get you. Bobby, Bobby, Bobby!"

With that, I turned and rode my bike away as fast as I could pedal. "White trash," I mumbled. "Damn, why do we have to be so poor?"

Bobby's folks moved to a different state. I never saw him again.

FIGHTING FOR FUN, 1940

Me and a few other boys, sitting on the steps of the Southside Baptist Church, held a spitting contest. The sidewalk in front of us showed dozens of dark spots where the spit hadn't dried yet under the hot July sun of St. Joseph, Missouri.

"My Grandpa chews tobacco," I said. "You should see him spit. We got wasps that live in the ground in our front yard. Grandpa sits on the porch and spits tobacco juice on 'em when they come out of the ground."

"Ain't he afraid of getting stung?"

"Course not. Me and my two sisters ain't afraid neither. We sit real still and the wasps come and light on our skin. We ain't never been stung yet. Grandpa taught us that. He ain't afraid of nothin'."

"Boy, you wouldn't catch me doin' that! I hate wasps and bugs and spiders."

"You couldn't live at my house then. We got all three of 'em and all kinds at that," I said. "'Specially in the cellar. I don't like goin' down there."

"Hey! Look at how far I can spit!" said Norm. He threw his head forward as he spit and landed further than anyone else had.

"You cheated!" I yelled. "You moved your head. Besides, you're standin' on the wrong step. You're closer than anyone else."

"Don't you call me a cheat," warned Norm.

"I wouldn't call you one if you wasn't one."

"Oh, yeah?"

"Yeah!"

"Wanna make somethin' of it?"

"I can whip you any old time."

"I beat up on Mike. I'm ten and he's thirteen and I whipped him good."

"Betcha can't do it to me."

"Betcha I can. You have to hit me first, though. Daddy said I can't never start a fight, but I can't ever run away from one neither."

"Where do you want me to hit you?" asked Norm.

On my shoulder."

Both of us moved out to the green grass between the sidewalk and street. The other boys gathered around us in a circle, egging us on.

"Well," I said, "you gonna hit me or not?"

The preacher came out to get into his car parked across the street. "What's going on here?" he demanded. "You boys would be better off inside the church instead of on the steps in front of it. You quit that spitting, you hear?"

"Yes, sir," came the chorus. We broke formation and waited until he drove away.

"You still wanna fight?" asked Norm.

"I don't care," I said.

"Me, neither," said Norm.

"Well, I do," said Clay, the biggest and heaviest kid of the lot. "Who wants to fight me?"

"Not me," came another chorus.

"What about you, Jack?" asked Clay.

"Yeah, Jack. Go ahead," said the group.

"We ain't got nothin' to fight about," I said.

"Oh, yeah? Where'd you get those rabbit teeth and big ears? Your mama a jackass? Your daddy a rabbit?"

I felt myself flush. "Don't you talk about my mother. She's dead."

"Jackass, jackass, son of a mule."

"Shut up!" I rushed him. Clay sidestepped and hit me in the side of the head, throwing me off balance. I recovered quickly and used the same windmill technique I'd used on Mike. It worked, but not before I got a black eye and Clay, a bloody nose. We quit fighting at the same time, neither of us a clear-cut winner.

"Boy! You sure do know how to hit!" said Clay, holding his nose.

"You too," I said, holding my eye.

"Shake and make up?" asked Clay, holding out his hand.

"Sure," I said and took the offered palm.

"I got into a fight today," I told my dad that night as he looked sharply at my face.

"Yeah, I see you did. What did I tell you about fighting?"

"Not to."

"Who started it?"

"He did."

"You whup him?"

"No, sir. We came out even, but he's bigger than me."

"What was it about?"

I was leery about the name calling. "Spittin," I said. I told him most of the rest of the story and he laughed when I was done.

"Well, I ain't sayin' as how I approve, but I'm sure glad you ain't no chicken. You gonna have to fight him again?"

"Nope. We're best friends now."

"Well, if that don't beat all!"

"How come?" I asked.

"Here I teach you not to fight and you go ahead and fight anyway and make the guy that give you a black eye your best friend. That ain't what fightin's supposed to be about."

"Maybe fightin's different for kids than it is for grownups."

He looked surprised. "Yeah, son. Maybe it is…maybe it is."

VIRGINIA

I missed my mother a lot, in spite of trying not to. Dad used to scold me more than he spanked me. Even when I got spanked, Mom would always make him stop before I got hurt too bad. Now, though, he hit me more than he scolded me. I always cried, but half the tears were for the pain, the other half, for missing Mom.

Staying at Grandma's house while Dad was at work was a mixture of fun and ugly. It was fun to be able to do whatever we wanted to outside because Grandma couldn't get outside in her wheelchair. My sisters and I would crawl under the front and back porches and play games all the time. It was our own nest that grownups couldn't come to.

Carrying Grandma's slop jar out to the outhouse, though, was an ugly job. The smell was always sickening.

One day, I heard Grandma complaining to Grandpa about the extra work caused by us kids. She told him she was going ask Dad to do something about it. I told my sisters and all three of us got worried right away. I decided to eavesdrop. Grandma and Grandpa were in the kitchen, so I turned out the light in my room and pushed the door open just enough to both see and hear.

"Joe, the kids mean the world and all to me, but I'm just not in any shape to handle them day after day," she said when he came to pick us up after work.

"Well, dammit, Ma, I just don't know what else I can do. I've gotta work to feed, house, and clothe them. I sure as hell can't take them to the job with me. You tell me what I should do."

"I don't know, Joe. All I know is I can't keep this up much longer."

"Well, I've got me an idea. The only thing I can do is find 'em a new mother."

"You hush your mouth! You ain't ever gonna find them kids a new mother. Zina's not cold in her grave yet and you talkin' like that. Shame on you."

"Shame or no, I sent my picture to every woman I ever knew tellin' 'em I'm in bad need of a wife."

"A wife's one thing; a mother's another."

"Sorry, Ma. I meant no disrespect to Zina. It's just that they need a woman's hand in their lives. Matter of fact, I'm askin' Buck Akron for Virginia's hand tonight."

"Virginia! She's a baby herself! How old is she, sixteen?"

"She's seventeen."

"And you're thirty. How long do you think that would last?"

"That'd be up to her. She's a good, church-goin' woman, and she loves the kids. She told me so."

"Does she love you?"

"That don't make no difference."

Grandpa, listening in silence, finally broke in. He got double joy out of being obscene. He loved to shock his audience and he loved to upset Granma. It was his way of getting even with her for denying him her bed.

"You sure know how to pick 'em, Joe. That Virginia's prime meat. You laid her yet?"

Dad blushed. "I ain't laid a finger on her. We've just talked, that's all."

"She a virgin, like her name says?"

"Says so. I don't know. What difference does it make? She'd be good for the kids. That's all I care about. You know how hard it is on Ma."

"It ain't nearly as hard on her as she makes it out to be. She loves Jack, tolerates Jeannine, and hates Donna," said Grandpa.

"I don't hate Donna!" protested Granma. "I just don't like the way she was conceived, that's all."

"Well, what the hell do you know about that, Ma?"

"I can count nine months backwards. She was conceived on your birthday after you and Mr. Smith got drunk in this very kitchen. If she hadn't been born, if you hadn't rode Zina to an early grave, you wouldn't be huntin' for a woman now."

"Now, that ain't fair, Ma. Zina had as much to do with it as I did. She was a lusty woman, you know. Sometimes she wouldn't leave me be until I did it to her."

"You shut up about Zina! Take your kids and get out of here. I don't want to hear you no more."

"All right, Ma, all right. Come on you kids. Let's go home."

Buck Akron sat on his side of the front porch, picking out "Old Joe Clark" on his banjo.

"Evenin, Buck."

"Evenin', Joe."

"Buck, I came to ask for Virginia's hand in marriage."

Buck plunked a few chords. "You get right to the point, don't you, Joe?"

"We've talked about it. Even talked about runnin' away. But I ain't made like that. She needs, we need, your permission."

"Ain't got her in trouble, have you?"

"No, ain't nothin' like that. My kids need a mother and she loves my kids."

"Well, I ain't got no wife neither. I need her here at home."

"She'd only be right next door. I ain't goin' nowhere."

"Don't know, Joe. What does she say about it?"

"Why don't you ask her?"

"Virginia! Get on out here!"

She came at once. She'd been listening just inside the door.

"Yes, Papa?"

"You fixin' to marry Joe?"

"Yes, Papa."

"He ain't got you in no trouble, has he?"

"No, Papa."

"You wanna marry him?"

"Yes, Papa."

"What about his kids?"

"I got real kindly feelin's for his young 'uns, Papa."

"What about me?"

"I'd only be right next door. I'd still fix your supper and I could do all the laundry at the same time."

"Cleanin' too?"

"Yes, Papa."

"Zina lived there when she died, you know."

"I know. It don't matter."

"Well, alright then. I reckon you got my blessin'."

Buck picked up his banjo and began a lively playing of "She'll Be Comin' Round the Mountain". Joe and Virginia started dancing to it, both grinning widely at their easy success.

They were married the following week. No one but the witnesses attended—Virginia's brother and a guy from Dad's work. They were married at the J.P.'s office after work.

I never liked Virginia. The two girls got along okay with her but I felt she was a poor substitute for my real mother. Every night I would sneak out of bed and listen at their closed bedroom door. I couldn't completely understand what they were saying, but I could tell they weren't happy.

"Virginia, honey, a husband's got rights."

"Rights or no, Joe, I'm havin' my period and I don't want you atouchin' me."

"Just how long do you mean to make me wait?"

"I don't know. Wait 'til my period is over. Then we'll see."

Seven nights later, I heard Virginia scream. I barely got out of the way before she came crashing out of the door in her nightgown. She ran out of the back of our half and into the back of Buck's half of the tenement. Dad came stumbling after, trying to get his pants on and run at the same time. I went back to bed but couldn't get to sleep. I heard them arguing next door. It went on for a long time. I finally nodded off. The next thing I knew, Dad was waking us up.

"Come on, you kids. We're goin' to Grandma's house."

I never saw Virginia again. Buck said she'd gone to her own mom and filed for an annulment.

Grandpa thought it was hilarious. He slapped his thigh and cackled loudly as he listened to the story. Grandma just sat there, shaking her head and throwing mean glances at him. Dad had tears in his voice as well as his eyes.

"Honest to God, Ma, I never even got to touch her. She wouldn't let me. Said she was willin' to be a mother but didn't see as how she could be a wife to someone as old as me. Hell, Ma, I ain't all that old."

"I knew no good would come of this. What do you intend to do now?"

"Well, you remember all those pictures I sent out? One girl answered. Geraldine X."

"Geraldine! Why she must weigh three hundred pounds if she weighs an ounce!"

"Sure that ain't too much woman for you to handle, Joe?" asked Grandpa and busted into another fit of laughter.

"I can handle her just fine," said Joe. "At least she's old enough to know what it's all about."

"Have you talked to her yet?" asked Sarah.

"As a matter of fact, I have. We could move in with her parents. Mr. X already said we could share expenses. Then we'd move to a farm and share the work. Jack's old enough to help with the chores, feedin' the chickens, sloppin' the hogs, and milkin' the cows. I'd stay on my WPA job and Mr. X would work full time on the farm. His boy, Jimmy, could help out after school doin' some of the heavier work. Gerry knows all about Virginia and she don't care. She's a good woman."

"She a church woman?" asked Grandma.

"Well, as a matter of fact, no. None of 'em care much about church. But she's been baptized and that means she's been saved, so I don't see no cause for trouble."

"Saved for what?" asked Grandpa. "Saved for your bed?" He laughed again.

"Saved for the Lord," snapped Grandma.

"The Lord don't want to marry her; Joe does. I'd sure like to see their wedding night. Bet he sticks it in a wrinkle. Bet she'll look just like a fat old sow when a blind boar gets done with her. Jisum all over her ass." He laughed some more.

"Joe, you take your kids and get on home. Mr. Smith and I are about to have some words."

"Sure, Ma, sure. We'll see you tomorrow."

"Good night, Joe."

COW

       Dad, Gerry, Mr. and Mrs. X., their son, Jimmy, and us three kids all lived cramped together in a two-bedroom house in the city for two months until they got their farm deal made. It was a relief for all of us to move to the old but spacious two-story farmhouse. Even so, there wasn't enough space in the house for all of us, so Jimmy and I slept in the same bed in a room above the garage.

       I loved the chores. They made me feel like a man. I loved to spend my free time roaming the ten acres, exploring the sumac woods and shooting my BB gun at frogs in the creek.

       One day, I got up nerve enough to ask Dad where babies came from. Dad squatted down and put his arms around me.

       "Have you watched what the chickens and geese do?"

       "Sure I have. Lots of times."

       "Well, that's what people do too and that's where babies come from."

       "Oh."

       "Ain't it time to feed the chickens?"

       "Sure, Daddy."

       I had no idea what the chickens and geese did so I asked Jimmy.

       "A man and a woman, they get together. He puts his thing in her and nine months later, there's a baby. Haven't you noticed how big Gerry's belly is? She's gonna have a baby in about three months."

       I considered her bulk, decided I hadn't noticed any change and shut up. That very night, Jimmy tried to put his thing in my rear end. I didn't mind. I just pretended like I was asleep and listened to Jimmy masturbate after he failed to achieve entry. In adulthood, I learned that he also raped Jeannine and Donna.

       The next morning, I felt a special bond to Jimmy. I thought it gave me special rights. Jimmy's pants were thrown on the bed so I went through the pockets. I found some coins and an almost full package of gum. I took them.

       Jimmy squealed on me. Dad was furious that I could be a thief. He stripped me naked that night in the garage and began beating me with a heavy leather belt. I felt betrayed and undeserving of the punishment, so I yelled every time the leather landed. It wasn't until the first seven or eight licks had landed that the pain really settled in. The yells became screams and only caused Dad to hit harder and faster.

Finally, the women came out of the house and made him stop. Jimmy tried to comfort me that night, saying he was sorry, but I would have none of it. I slept fitfully and awoke sore and bruised and filled with a dislike for all that the farm represented.

The next week, Mr. X. brought home a cow in the back of the farm truck. He told me to milk her after he off-loaded her into the barn and put her in the stanchion. Half-an-hour later, he came back to see how much milk she had given. There was none in the bucket.

"You ain't worth the powder and lead to blow you to Hell."

I stood trembling as Mr. X. roared those words down upon me. I tried not to flinch but failed. The words came as if from the realm of God, Himself, raining down terror upon the already helpless.

"What's the matter? You afraid of getting hurt? I'll show you what hurt is."

A head-rolling slap followed. Anger and hurt fought for my face. Hurt won. Instead of snarling, I sniveled. I hadn't milked the cow because she was a young heifer that was ready to milk for the first time. When I tried, trusting that she would be as docile as the older cow, she kicked me clear across the barn.

"Can'tcha even milk a god dam cow? Ain'tcha got any brains at all? You gotta put your head in her flank and stand out so's she can't reach you with her hooves. I'm going to show you what happens to cows that kick. I'm goin' to get your dad. You stay in the barn."

"What's goin' on in there?" I heard my dad's voice bellow in that special way that I knew was for Mr. X's benefit. The fear of a beating dried up my tears. I retrieved the milk bucket and stuck my head in the cow's flank just as Mr. X. and Dad appeared in the doorway. I relaxed and the cow kicked me again. I landed in the corner, inhaling the strange perfume of cow dung, urine, and hay.

"Dumb," said Mr. X., "just plain dumb."

Dad didn't ask me if I was hurt. He just stood there and glowered at me. "What are you going to do?" asked Dad.

"Beat some sense into her god-damn head. I want your boy to watch. He's gettin' to be a fuckin' sissy. Put the shackles on that heifer."

As Dad approached the cow to obey, she started prancing her hind end back and forth trying to free her head. Mr. X. picked up a piece of two-by-four longer than a baseball bat and started hitting her in the head. She began bellowing, a grown-up but calf-like bawling that sounded to me like my own terror. The beating made her stop prancing and Dad slipped the hobbles on. They were made of U-shaped steel that slipped over her hamstrings. Connected by a chain, they prevented her from moving a leg forward more than a few inches.

"There," said Mr. X. "By the time I'm finished with her, she'll learn not to kick."

He poked her udder with the two-by-four. She tried to kick. He kicked her back with his steel-toed work shoes, not once, but over and over. He poked and kicked until he was panting and she was no longer bellowing. Then he went after her again with the two-by-four, hitting her with full, swinging blows all over her body, talking to her, cussing and shouting about kicking over the milk pail. When he was done, the cow was on her knees, half-strangled in the stanchion, the two-by-four broken into two pieces. He picked up a slat from the corner when I stood frozen, photographing everything I saw, smelled, and heard.

"You get on over there and get ready to milk this cow," he ordered me. "Take those shackles off, Joe." Then he started beating the cow on her nose with the slat. "Get up, you stinkin' heifer."

Dad held the bucket out. "Here, son." Then he turned to Mr. X. "You sure do know how to tame them, Dad. She won't give us anymore trouble."

My hands trembled as I took the bucket and stuck my head in the cow's flank.

"Boy, Mr. X.!" said Joe. You sure know how to tame 'em! Look at my boy go! Thataway son. Don't quit. Don't ever, ever quit."

FROG

Jimmy was already getting dressed when I awoke. "Mornin' Jack."

"Good mornin', Jimmy. How come you're gettin' up so early?"

"It ain't early, only eight o'clock. Gotta go to work. You're lucky. You don't have to pay room and board like I do."

"Can't you stay and play with me? I get tired of playin' with Jeannine and Donna. They only wanna play girls games. I'm lonesome for someone to play with."

"Sorry, kid. Maybe Sunday. Gotta go. Bye."

"Bye, Jimmy."

I lay in bed for a little while before getting up. I saw my BB gun in the corner of the room. Naked, I got up and retrieved it. I swung it around at targets: the knobs on the chest of drawers, a peeled spot of paint on the wall, a spot on the window where a spider had been smashed. "Bang!" I yelled at each target.

"Jack, you up yet?" Dad was yelling up from the driveway at the room above the garage.

"I'm up!" I shouted out the window.

"Well, get busy and feed the chickens."

"Ok, Dad, soon's I get my clothes on."

I dressed quickly, slipping into my shorts and bib overalls. I put on darned socks and adjusted the thick parts so they wouldn't hurt my feet. My tennis shoes, both of them worn out at the toes and frayed at the heels, I put on without untying.

I knew the animals had to be fed before I could eat so I hurried out to the barn, filled a pail with feed and threw it in handfuls over the chicken wire fence to the clucking hens and greedy geese. I was hungry this morning so I didn't wait to watch them eat and squabble over grains of corn.

"You wash up?" Dad asked when I entered the kitchen.

"Sorry," I said and went to the kitchen sink with the chipped-out white porcelain. A few strokes of the hand pump filled the also chipped-out blue porcelain wash basin. I spluttered my face into the cold water, washed my hands, and dried off on the towel made out of a flour sack. Although faded from many washings and bleachings, Quaker Feed Mill could still be read on it.

"You hungry?" asked Gerry.

"Starved," I said.

"We got biscuits and pan gravy. How many you want?"

"Fourteen."

"Suppose we start you out with four, then, if you want more, you can have 'em."

"Thanks, Gerry."

I cut the biscuits with my fork, sopped up gravy, and ate almost without stopping. When my plate was empty, I asked for four more.

"Here's two. If you still want more, you can have 'em," said Gerry.

"Dad, can I go huntin' today?"

"Huntin' for what?"

"Frogs. I'm tired of playin' with my sisters."

"Well, I reckon, but not until you've milked the cows. You havin' any more trouble with that heifer?"

Afraid of saying anything different for fear of causing more harm, I hesitated briefly. "No, sir. She's alright now." I continued the lie for my whole life for the same reason.

"Good. I gotta go to work. See you tonight, Gerry. So long, son."

I trudged over two sumac-covered hills to where the shallow creek flowed. I sneaked along the creek shore as I imagined my Cherokee ancestors might have done. My hope was to find a frog with legs big enough to eat. As I rounded a bend, there it was, sitting half in the water and half on shore, right at the bottom of a small dip in the creek bed. Moving with painful slowness, I took careful aim, pointing the muzzle down at the frog. The BB dribbled out of the muzzle before I could pull the trigger.

"Croak," went the frog as it heard the slight noise of the BB on the rocks Moving with minimum motion, I got another BB from my pocket, placed it in my mouth to get it wet, and transferred it from my lips into the muzzle opening. Again I took careful aim and pulled the trigger. Nothing happened. I'd forgotten to cock it. Flushing red by now, I stuck the muzzle in the air and carefully pulled the cocking lever.

"Croak," went the frog as it heard the noise. Then it moved.

I took quick aim and pulled the trigger. The BB hit where the frog had been. I could still see it though. Abandoning every thought of stealth, I tried to hit it with the butt of the BB gun, swinging it by its barrel like a club. The frog jumped, the stock of the gun shattered on the rocks, and I immediately felt sick in the pit of my stomach. It was the only gun I had and the only one I had any hope of ever owning. Rage welled up in me and I began pounding the BB gun into pieces against the rocks, cussing like I'd heard Mr. X. cuss when he beat the cow. As quickly as the rage began, it ended, and I started the long walk back to the farmhouse, shoulders down, feet dragging in the dust.

"Dang it. Dang it. Dang it," I said to the sumac bushes. "Why do I have to get so mad? All I hurt was my own dumb self. Now I ain't got no frog and no BB gun neither. Dang it. Dang it. Dang it."

"How would you like to earn some money, son?" asked Dad one evening at the dinner table.

"Who, me?" I said in surprise.

"You ain't no owl. Your feet don't fit no limb. Yes, you. The apple orchard needs pickers. You can pick the windfalls and low branches and get a dime a bushel. How does that sound?"

"Could I get enough to earn a new BB gun?"

"Don't see why not, provided you work hard and don't eat everything you pick."

"Aw, Dad."

"What do you say?"

"Sure!"

"We start this weekend."

"Can't we start right now? How long before I can buy a BB gun?"

"Well, let's see. I reckon a new gun oughtta be about five dollars. That's fifty bushels. If you work hard and don't dawdle, you oughtta be about two weekends at it."

"Fifty bushels! I don't reckon I could ever pick that many. Goll."

Dad looked at my fallen face before answering. "If you don't think you can, you never will."

"Yes, but, gee whiz, fifty bushels!"

"You pick 'em a peck at a time, son. You know how many a peck is?"

"Not rightly."

"Well, a peck is about how many you can get into that wash basin. You fill that two hundred times and you got fifty bushels."

"Two hundred times! Goll!"

Dad smiled. "It's easier than it sounds, son. Eat your supper now. You're letting it get cold."

I never saw so many apples in my life. The first frost had come and gone and left the ground covered with fallen fruit. Dad handed me a picking basket.

"This here holds a peck. There's four pecks to a bushel. Every time you fill up a bushel basket over there, you get a dime. Think you can handle it?"

My mind focused on my BB gun. More than anything else, I wanted that gun. The endless rows of evenly spaced trees swam before my eyes. "I gotta do it", I thought, "I just gotta."

"You hear me, son? Think you can do it?"

Resolve flowed into my mind like a flood, washing away doubt and indecision. "Sure, Dad. I won't quit either, not even if I get tired. I want me that gun."

"That's a good boy, son. Have at it."

I went to work like it was fun…at first. Some of the windfalls were partly rotten. I made a game out of stepping on them, squashing their mushiness into pancakes, inhaling their suddenly sharp aromas. I tried jumping up for apples just out of reach, but the bumping of the picking bag made me stop. Soon, though, I found a rhythm that carried me down the long, long row, one tree at a time.

My work got slower and slower as I grew more and more tired. After half-a-day at it, the peck basket felt like it was a bushel, and the trips back to the unloading station became longer and longer. But I stuck to it. When dark forced an end to the full day's labor, I was glad, tired, hungry, and quite proud of myself. Dad was proud of me too.

"I'm proud of you, son. You worked like a real field hand today."

"How much do you reckon I made?"

"Oh, two or three dollars. Mr. Simpson's keepin' tally. He'll pay us when we're all done."

"Do we have to do it again tomorrow?"

"Nope. Mr. Simpson don't believe in workin' on Sunday."

"I reckon I'll sleep then. I sure am pure tired."

"Reckon I will too, son. Long's we're not late for breakfast."

"I'm hungry."

"Let's get on back to the house then."

We climbed into the farm truck. In spite of its backfires and noisy muffler, in spite of the worn-out seat with the spring sticking through, in spite of the bumpiness of the dusty gravel road, I was asleep before we reached home.

The next Saturday was a cold one. I put on a jacket but that wouldn't keep my feet warm. My worn-out, holey tennis shoes were almost as bad as being barefoot.

"My feet are gettin' cold," I complained to Dad about halfway through the day.

"Move a little faster, son. We'll be done before you know it. Might even be done before sunset."

I did but it didn't help much. The colder my feet got, the more the day seemed to drag out. But, finally, the apples were all picked and we were on the way home. In the kitchen, Dad tossed two envelopes on the table. They clunked from the coins in them.

"There it is, Gerry. Oughtta be enough in there to get you that new dress you been wantin'."

Gerry opened Dad's envelope first and counted the bills and change. "Sixteen dollars and sixty cents," she announced. "Let's see what Jack's got. Five dollars and fifty cents. Good work, Jack! Now we can buy you a new pair of Brogans."

"I want a BB gun," I said.

"No," said Gerry. "You need new shoes and that's that. Winter's comin' on and you ain't got nothin' decent for your feet."

"Dad?" I said. "Dad, you promised."

"Sorry, son, your mother's right. Shoes are more important. Maybe next year."

"She ain't my mother! I hate her! I hate you too!"

Dad backhanded me across the mouth. "You get the hell on up to your room until you can learn to keep a civil tongue in your mouth. Go on now. Get!"

Full again of fury, I ran to my room before anyone could see me crying. I slammed the door shut behind me, laid belly down on the bed, and let the tears go. When I was done, I sat up and looked a long time at the corner where my BB gun had been. Moved by a sudden idea, I went to the chest of drawers, opened Jimmy's drawer, and pulled out a hunting knife in its sheath. Then, without untying them, I took off my tennis shoes and stood them in the BB gun corner. Backing off to my bed, I unsheathed the knife. I stared for a while at its shiny surfaces, turning it around and over, testing the point against my palm. Suddenly I grasped it at the tip and threw it hard at my shoes.

"Field hand," I hissed.

The knife clattered harmlessly to the smooth pine floor. Three more times I threw it.

"Field hand, field hand, field hand. Lousy damned field hand."

Three more times, the knife failed to stick. The final time, I retrieved the shoes along with the knife, took them to my bed and coldly, methodically, cut them to pieces.

QUARREL

The apple tree behind the garage was just right for my sisters to climb. Jeannine loved to spend hours in it, listening to birds and farm noises, and watching the geese roam around. Donna was inside the farmhouse this day, grounded for disobeying one of Gerry's rules. I was playing in the garage with the tools that were there. Dad arrived home from work.

"Hi, Son!"
"Hi, Dad!"
"What are you doin' in there?"
"Playin'."
"You be sure and put everything back just like you found it."
"Ok, Dad. Donna can't come out today."
"Why not?"
"I dunno. Gerry won't let her."
"You can call her mother, if you want to."
"I don't want to."

Dad sighed and entered the house. It wasn't long until I heard him and Gerry screaming at each other. I made out some of the words.

"I ain't gonna darn your god-damned kids' socks anymore!"

"God-damned kids, huh? You knew I had kids when you married me! Just because you're pregnant doesn't give you any special rights, you know. My kids are entitled to a woman in their lives. That means cookin', laundry, and mendin'. I can't afford to be buyin' 'em new things all the time."

"When's the last time you ever bought 'em anything new? Jack bought his own Brogans with his apple orchard money. That's the only thing new I ever did see him get."

"Well, maybe the kids are too much for you. Maybe you're not woman enough to handle 'em."

"Well, maybe not!"
"Maybe you ain't woman enough to handle me, neither."
"Fat chance of that, you shrimp."
"Well, I know where the kids will be appreciated."
"Well, why don't you take 'em there, then?"
"By God, I will!" Dad came out with Donna in his arms. "Jack, go and get Jeannine. We're going to Grandma's."

I knew better than to ask any questions. I ran to the apple tree. "Jeannine, Dad wants us. He's takin' us to Grandma's."

"How come?"

"He and Gerry's been fightin' again. I'm scared."

"Me too." She swung down from the tree and we went to the front of the garage. Gerry was pushing Dad away from the truck. She pushed the lock button down and slammed the door shut.

"Joe, you ain't agoin' nowhere."

"Give me the keys."

"They're locked inside the truck. Please, Joe, I didn't mean it."

"Well, that ain't gonna stop me. Come on, you kids."

Carrying Donna, he made long strides down the driveway. Jeannine and I had to trot to keep up. We entered the clay and gravel road that went for a mile until it hooked up to the blacktop. Once on the highway, he started hitchhiking as we walked. A farm truck pulled up and stopped. He put all three of us in the backend and he climbed into the passenger seat.

"Much obliged, Henry."

"Where you headin'?"

"To Grandma Smith's house. Me and Gerry split up."

"I'll take you there. Ain't more than a mile outta my way."

"Much obliged, Henry. Much obliged."

"What's the matter?" Jeannine asked me.

"Dad's takin' us to Grandma's. He and Gerry had a fight."

"Looks like Dad lost," she said.

"Looks to me like us kids lost," I said. "We ain't got no home again."

All of us kept quiet then, lost in our private fears. What if Grandma wouldn't take us in? What if she would?

"Please, Ma. You gotta keep the kids for a little while until Gerry and I work things out."

"I don't have to do no such thing," said Grandma.

"Ha, ha, ha, ha, ha! I knew she was too much of a woman for you!" cackled Grandpa. "How long you 'spect it'll be?"

"A few days, two weeks, maybe. Gerry despises havin' the kids around. She's a little touchy, bein' pregnant and all."

"I oughtta send you and the kids right back to her, that's what I oughtta do," said Grandma.

"Who's gonna pay for their feed," asked Grandpa.

Dad took out his billfold and pulled out a twenty-dollar bill. "This oughtta do for a week," he said.

Grandpa came over quickly and took the bill before Grandma could get to it. "Ok," said Grandpa, "a week, no more…'less, of course, you got more where that came from."

"You give me that money, Mr. Smith. I don't want it spent on whiskey. That's for the kids' food bill."

"I'll take care of the vittles. Don't you worry none."

Grandma raised her palms above her head. "I give up," she said. "A body's just got so much fight in 'em and I'm plumb tuckered out. Joe, you do what you have to do. I'll take care of the kids while you take care of your wife. Are you gonna stay awhile or do you have to get back?"

"Got a jug of wine, Joe," tempted Grandpa.

"Naw. Thanks anyway. I gotta hitchhike back and I'd just as soon do it before dark."

"All right, Joe," said Sarah. "You keep in touch."

"Now, how can I do that, Ma? Ain't neither of us got a phone. Reckon you'll just have to trust that I'm doin' the best I can."

"Well, don't let it be too long. Kids need a father, too."

"All right Ma, all right. Goodbye."

The week dragged on for three weeks, then a month. Not a word was heard from Dad. My sisters and I had talked about it until we were afraid to ask any more questions, not even to each other. Grandma was worried too. At the kitchen table one night, she brought it up. Supper was one of my favorites, chicken and dumplings, but as soon as the subject started, I quit eating and just listened. Jeannine did too. Donna was too young to understand so she kept on eating.

"Dad," Grandma said to Grandpa, "do you reckon you could go out to the farm and talk to Joe. The kids are eatin' us out of house and home and I just don't know how we can put up with it much longer. School starts in two weeks; the kids ain't even got a change of clothes and I'm at my wit's end."

"It sure does beat all how he just dropped out of sight. I can't go out there, though. That dusty road would have my asthma kickin' up somethin' fierce. Do you reckon we could write to him?"

"Well, I don't know. If he ain't payin' any mind to 'em now, I 'spect he wouldn't pay no mind to a letter. Somethin's gotta be done, Mr. Smith, and you're the only one able-bodied enough to do it. Maybe one of your cronies at the bar could drive you out there?"

"Well, now, maybe. You got any money? I'll go down to the bar and see."

Grandma looked at him sharply, then sighed and took two dollars out of the small purse she hid under the seat cushion of her wheelchair. "Don't you come back drunk," she ordered.

"Can't get drunk on two dollars," he said. "Besides, I'll be treatin' whoever can take me out."

"Well, go on then, before they get too drunk to know what they're sayin'."

Grandpa kept up a steady stream of chatter on the way to the farmhouse. He told Grandma all about it when he got back.

"John," he said, "I sure hope he's home. I got a thing or two on my mind. Sure beats all hell how a man can run away and desert three little kids just like they was unwanted cats.

"I remember when he married my daughter. She got sickly just after the second one was born. Doc told him not to have any more. Didn't listen. Got drunk on his birthday and knocked her up again. That wasn't enough. Had to go and knock her up again after that. She died in childbirth with that one. His name was Jerry Dale. Buried him right in her arms in the same casket.

"John, you just don't know what it's like to lose your only daughter to a man's balls. Sarah blames me. Says I got him drunk. Hell, man, he got himself drunk. Sarah won't let up on me, though."

"Take a right just past the schoolhouse. It's about a mile more."

"I reckon I'll burn his ears for him. Shoulda brung the kids with us. Dump 'em off just like he did. Sarah wouldn't hear of it though. 'Spite of all her bitchin', she loves them kids."

"Here we are. Don't you run off on me now."

Grandpa got out and pounded on the screen door. Gerry's three-hundred pound bulk filled the doorway. She made no effort to invite him in.

"What the hell are you doin' here?"

"Come to see Joe. Have to talk to him about his kids."

"Well, you cain't see Joe. He's done gone and joined the Army Air Corps."

"You're lyin'."

"You got no call to talk to me that way! He run away from me and joined up. Said he could get an education. I only heard from him twice. For Christ's sake, he wasn't even here to see his daughter get borned. I'm supposed to get an allotment but I ain't seen one dime yet. You want to see Joe, you go to San Antone, Texas."

"Well, I'll be damned. You got room for his kids?"

"No, I ain't got no room for his god-damned brats. I got all I can handle with the baby."

"Well, it seems to me you got a responsibility to 'em."

"No, I ain't got no responsibility to 'em. That's your problem."

"You got an address for Joe?"

"You wait here. I'll give you an envelope with his return address on it."

"Much obliged."

She came back quickly. "Here. Now you go away and don't come back. I don't want to see or hear from you, Mrs. Smith, or those kids ever again. You understand me?"

"I reckon I do. Goodbye, Ma'am."

"Goodbye!"

Grandpa got back into John's car. He was silent all the way back home.

DRESS

	Jeannine and I knew there was something wrong the instant we came home from school. We didn't come home with each other but we got there at the same time anyway. When we came in the front door, Grandma had her wheelchair at the round oak table and was reading her Bible. We knew enough not to interrupt her. She always read her Bible when she was upset about something. We figured it must have been Donna, because she'd been home from school three days sick. In spite of Grandma saying she loved all of us, we knew she practically hated Donna, blaming her birth for speeding up Momma's death.
	We went straight into the room Jeannine and Donna shared. It was a small room, made by putting up a flimsy partition in a regular-sized room, just like my room was. Donna sat on the bed, feet on the floor, eyes red from crying, shoulders slumped way down.
	"What happened?" I asked. She didn't answer. Jeannine sat beside her and put her arm around her shoulders.
	"What's wrong, honey?" Did Grandma do somethin' to you?" All she did was nod. I knew Grandma would be able to hear us talking where we were.
	"Come on in my room," I said. "She can't hear us in there."
	I went at once. Right behind, Jeannine led Donna in. Once inside, I shut the door, put the radio on and placed it by the door so no one could hear us. Jeannine and Donna sat on my cot. I sat on the floor in front of them, my back against the wall.
	"Was Grandma mean to you again?" asked Jeannine.
	"She did the meanest thing she's ever done to me," said Donna. She was trying hard to keep her voice under control. "You know Mrs. Holcomb, the woman Grandma does sewin' for?"
	We both nodded yes.
	"Well, she bought me a new dress..."
	"Mrs. Smith," she said, "I hope you don't mind, but I bought a new dress that seemed to be just the right size for Donna. It was on sale and I don't miss the money, so I hope you'll let her have it."
	"We don't accept no charity in this house. We may be poor but we're proud."
	"This isn't charity, it's a gift; a gift of love. Doesn't the Good Book say to give of ourselves to those less fortunate? Jesus Christ would approve of this, you know."
	"Well, if you put it that way...."

"That's better. Can we see if it fits?"
"I suppose so. Donna! Get in here!"

"I didn't do nothin', Grandma."
"I know you didn't. Mrs. Holcomb brought you a new dress. She wants to see if it fits. Take off what you're awearin'."

Donna couldn't believe it. "A new dress? For me? I ain't never had a new dress." "Well, quit your lollygaggin' and slip it on."

She was quick about it, believe you me. "Ohh, it's so pretty," Donna said. "I just love the colors. Can I see what it looks like in the mirror?"

"Of course you can, dear," said Mrs. Holcomb before Grandma could answer.

"Use the dressin' table mirror in my room," said Grandma.

She looked at herself and laughed out loud. She even thought she looked pretty.

"All right, that's enough now," said Grandma. "Take it off and hang it in the closet."

"Can't I wear it just a little while?"

"No, you can't just wear it a little while. You can wear it to church and that's all."

"But Grandma...."

"Don't but me. Take it off...right now." She took it off as slow as she could. She touched the pretty colored flowers on it one by one. "Quit dawdlin'! Mrs. Holcomb doesn't have all day."

"You're right, Mrs. Smith. I have to be going now."

"Donna, ain't you even got the common courtesy to say thank you."

"Thank you, Mrs. Holcomb."
"It's my pleasure, child. Wear it in good health."
"I will, Mrs. Holcomb. Thank you again."
"Goodbye, dear. Goodbye, Mrs. Smith."

Donna was still playin' with the flowers after Mrs. Holcomb left.

"Put it away," said Grandma.
"Do I hafta? I want to show it to Jack and Jeannine."
"You put it away like I said," said Grandma, starting to get mad.

"Pleeease?"

"Don't please me, you brat! You ain't never pleased me yet and I don't expect you ever will. You put that dress away right now."

"It's my dress," she said. "Mrs. Holcomb gave it to me, not you."

Grandma got furious. "You snot-nosed little brat! I'll teach you to smart off to me!"

Grandma picked up a yardstick. She hit her with it every time she came close enough. It didn't matter which part of her she hit. She hit her head, legs, arms, chest, it didn't matter. The yardstick swished through the air and smacked as it hit. Donna dodged and tried to hide behind whatever she could but it didn't do any good. The way Grandma had the furniture arranged for her wheelchair, there was nothing to hide behind. The more Donna cried, the madder Grandma got.

Donna finally got tired of trying. She stopped crying and stepped out into the middle of the room and hid her face in her hands. She stood still as Grandma beat welts onto her. Grandma got even madder because Donna wouldn't cry. Then, the yardstick broke. Right away, she went to her sewing machine and got out a pair of scissors. She picked up the new dress off the floor and cut it into pieces right before Donna's eyes. It was like her whole insides just let go and fell down. Then she told Donna to go to her room and stay there.

Jeannine got furious. I tried to think of some way to help Donna not to feel so bad.

"You'll get another dress, Donna," I said. "When I get a job, I'll buy you lots of pretty clothes."

"Grandma's a cruel, old woman," said Jeannine. "I wish she'd die. I wish Daddy'd come back. Do you think he's ever gonna come back, Jack?"

"Sure he will. As soon as the war's over. Remember how he taught us never to quit? He'll come back and take us kids back. Then we won't be poor anymore. We'll have things like the rest of the kids. Don't you worry. He'll be back."

LETTER

Grandma and Grandpa fought faithfully on the first of every month. Course, they fought all month long, too, but this one was always about money. His Spanish-American War pension came then and he always wanted half of it to go get drunk on. Grandma always held out and he'd wind up with ten dollars. Dad's money order for twenty-five dollars came about the fifth. They never fought about that, but both of them would bad mouth Dad for not sending more and not writing.

"He don't know if his kids are alive and well or sick and dead," complained Grandma.

I never let on how bad that made me feel. I never knew if he was sick or dead neither. One day, it was different.

"Dad," said Grandma, "Joe has sent us a letter."

"Well, I'll be damned. First one in over three years. What'd he have to say?"

I was in my little room reading. When I heard "Joe" and "letter", my ears practically swiveled to hear more. I laid down my book and moved to the doorway where I could hear without being seen.

"I don't reckon I can read it. I spent half an hour at the five-and-dime pickin' a new pair of glasses out of their bin but there just weren't none that fit me. Here, you read it."

"Any money in it?"

"Just the twenty-five dollars."

"Dear Mom and Dad: Hope you and the kids are well. I'm gettin' discharged this month and will stop by to pick the kids up. Yours truly, Joe."

A thrill went through me from head to toe. I even got dizzy and had to close my eyes and hold on tight to stay up straight. At last, at long, long last, my dad was coming to get us out of this hellhole. No more hand-me-downs. No more lard sandwiches. No more being ashamed of where we lived. No more, no more, no more.

"Well, don't that beat all," said Grandma. "He expects us just to give the kids back and call it even."

"He'll play hell gettin' those kids back. Not after all we had to go through to get guardianship of 'em so we could draw ADC.

I felt the bottom of the earth fall out through my stomach. I didn't know about no guardianship. I knew the ACD lady came to visit sometimes but I never knew why. They always sent us outside to play. Guardianship? What the hell did that mean? He was still our daddy.

"He'll get us back, all right," I whispered. "He'll just knock you down and take us if he has to."

"Well," said Grandma, "that's up to you to handle. If I never see him again, it will be too soon. He rode our daughter to death, abandoned his kids on us, and he expects...dear Jesus. You do what you have to do, Mr. Smith. I have to make out the grocery order. Twenty-five dollars a month for three hungry kids."

She wheeled to the kitchen table, picked up a tablet and stub of a pencil and began to write. She spotted me out of the corner of her eye.

"You hear me say your daddy's comin' back?"

"No!" I said, acting surprised. "When?"

"Didn't say," said Grandpa. "Don't matter none. He ain't getting' you."

"Why not? He's our daddy?"

"Not no more, he ain't. We had to take out guardianship papers on all three of you so's we could collect ADC."

"What's ADC?"

"Aid to Dependent Children. They help pay for kids that's been abandoned."

"We ain't been abandoned."

"Oh, you ain't, huh? How many times have you heard from your pa in the last four years? Not one word. Who put the clothes on your back, the food in your bellies and a roof over your head? Who paid the doctor bills? Who...?"

"All right, ok, but he went off to fight in the war."

"Fight, my ass. He never left the U.S. of A. He ain't man enough to fight. You might as well face up to it, Jack, your dad's a coward. He can't even face up the responsibilities he brought on himself."

All of a sudden, I felt mad clean through to my bones. My knees begun to shake like they wanted to run up to him and kick him to pieces.

"You hate my dad, don't you?"

"Damn right, I do. He's just plumb no good."

"Then I hate you too!" I screamed.

'Grandpa looked surprised but it was Grandma who spoke up.

"If you wasn't so big, I'd wash your mouth out with lye soap. Mr. Smith ain't the world's best, God only knows, but the least he's deservin' of is your respect. Now you apologize."

I didn't know what to say. Grandma never took Grandpa's part before. I knew I wasn't going to apologize, even though both of them were looking mean at me now. I tried to look mean back at them but I was too close to crying. I couldn't let them see me cry. God damned tears. Why'd God have to give boys tears? I went back inside my room and slammed the door shut. I turned up my radio as loud as it would go. Then I yelled back at them.

"Oh, yeah? You just wait and see! My daddy knows how to fight pretty good. He might even beat you up. Wait'll I tell Jeannine and Donna we don't hafta be poor anymore. Oh, God, please make it happen soon."

I felt the tears coming again. I started beating on my thigh. I beat on it until it was too sore to beat anymore.

SCHOOL

I was sitting in the swing on the front porch with Grandpa when Dad came back from the war. I didn't recognize him at first. He came walking down the street, still dressed in his soldier clothes. The direction he came from was the bus stop. I didn't know he was my dad until he turned in at the house.

"Daddy!" I yelled, just as Grandpa got up to meet him face-to-face. Dad didn't look at me or even say hello. Grandpa stood on the front porch barring the way. Dad stood three steps below on the ground. Dad spoke first.

"I come for my kids."

"They ain't your kids no more."

"They sure as hell are! What are you tryin' to pull?"

"I ain't pullin' nothin', Joe. You abandoned 'em. We had to get help. The only way we could do that was to go to Aid to Dependent Children. God knows the two-bits you sent every month wouldn't feed three hungry mouths. The ADC checked out that you abandoned your own kids and gave us guardianship. They ain't yours no more."

I went into shock. I hadn't known a thing about what Grandpa was saying. I expected my dad to knock him down and take us kids back anyway. He did nothing of the sort.

"You mean I got nothin' to say about it anymore?"

"That's right."

Dad turned on his heel and walked away without another word. He was at the furthest end of the block before I could find any voice at all.

"Don't quit!" I yelled. "Don't quit! Don't you dare quit!"

Dad turned the corner and I started running after him.

"Dad! Wait! Dad! Come back! Maybe Grandpa's wrong! Don't quit! Please don't quit!"

It was too late. I reached the corner just as the bus pulled away.

I felt no hope at all. I must really be bad if my own dad didn't want me. Maybe it was because I cried so much. I vowed never to cry again. I began to drink and use drugs. I stole the liquor, usually from Grandpa's plentiful supply of homemade wine. Sometimes, I would steal bottles of liquor from an understaffed drugstore. My family's favorite remedy for a cold was terpin hydrate with codeine. I stole that too. It wasn't long until I was playing hooky because I was hung over and sick from my excesses. My grades suffered from uncompleted work. The weeks dragged painfully by until, without notice, I quit school in the tenth grade.

Relatives and friends gathered around me, trying to find out what was wrong, hoping to change my mind, reminding me that I was their one great hope. I was to succeed, through education, where none of them had been able to succeed before. I was to bring a new pride, a new joy, to the family name. Nothing worked. I set out to find a job.

The first eight jobs I applied for all told me the same thing: I was too young. Finally, the truth about education became clear. Without an education, I was nothing.

A good six or seven weeks went by until I decided to go back to school. I had to have an interview with the principal first.

"Hello, Mr. Colter."

"Hello, Jack. I understand you want to come back."

"Yes, sir."

"You realize, of course, that you cannot rejoin your class. You'll have to be put back a year."

"Then I ain't comin' back."

Mr. Colter looked surprised at my defiance. All my school life, I'd been afraid of getting put back. It would just be too humiliating.

"I see," he said.

"No, you don't. The kids would laugh at me and point their fingers at me. I couldn't take that. If I can't graduate with my class, I won't graduate at all."

"Jack, your record shows that, in spite of being bright, you failed to work up to your potential. You almost never do homework and you're always staring out the window in classes. How do you expect to succeed?"

"Because I know better now. In order to get a good job, I gotta have an education."

"Just coming to school and attending classes won't give you an education. Education is hard work. It means homework, too, every day."

"I can do it."

"Well, we'll just see about that. I'm going to let you return to your class provided you make up all the work you missed. Do you think you can do that?"

"I know I can."

"I wish I were as sure as you are. You certainly have what it takes except, perhaps, ambition. Go ahead. Return to your class."

"Right now?"

"Right now."

"Yes, sir." I felt funny walking in the door of Miss Frye's class. The kids all looked at me and Miss Frye stopped teaching.

"Welcome back, Jack. Are you here for good?"

"Yes, ma'am. Can I please have a seat in the front row? I can see the blackboard better."

She moved a girl with glasses to a different seat and gave me hers. For the first time ever, I started making notes instead of wishing I was somewhere else.

GOLD STAR MOM, 1944

Carroll walked up to the porch were Grandpa sat spitting tobacco juice at ground hornets.

"Hi, Dad. I got some news. You wanna come in while I tell you about it?" Carroll handed Grandma a small package. "You're a Blue Star Mother now. I've joined the Army Air Corps." She opened the package and took out an eight-inch square of cotton, edged with a red fringe. A blue star on a white background filled the center. "You hang that in the window, Mom, so the whole world knows you got a son in the service."

"I don't want no son in the service."

"Ma, where's your patriotism? We're at war, you know."

"You got four babies! Are you crazy?"

"I report in two weeks."

I was on my bicycle a full block away when I saw the jeep drive up to the house. I raced back to the front yard and let it drop. Grandma was just opening the screen door as a man in a military uniform approached.

"Mrs. Smith?"

"Yes."

"I regret to inform you that your son, Carroll, was killed in the crash of his B-29 bomber on a training flight over Texas."

"Oh, my Lord."

"I'm sorry, Mrs. Smith. His body will be shipped back in a sealed coffin. There was a fire."

"Dear Jesus."

"What address would you like the coffin shipped to?"

"The Stauffer Funeral Home, I guess."

"Very well. I see you have a blue star in your window. I've brought you a new one, a gold star." The soldier opened the screen just enough to hand it to her. She took it casually, like it was a newspaper.

"I'll be in touch with you again when the body arrives. We'll see that he has a military funeral. I'm sorry, Mrs. Smith."

"Come on in here, Jackie. Come sit in my lap." I did. She stroked my hair and pulled my head close to her bosom. "You're all I have left now, Jackie. Promise me you'll never go to war."

"I promise, Grandma. Is Uncle Carroll really dead?"

I stayed on her lap for half an hour, not wanting to move, not daring to talk. Finally, she set me free and went to her bedroom.

I couldn't hear her words but, I knew she was praying both Christian and Cherokee prayers.

At the funeral, I was determined not to cry in front of everyone. I held out until they fired the rifles. The shots brought back all of the hunting Uncle Carroll had done with me; I broke down. I began crying for my loss and yelling at God for letting it happen. Grandpa came quickly to me.

"Don't cry, Jack. It can't be helped. We all have to die. You have to be strong, son, stronger than all the things that have hurt you. If you're not, you'll be of no help to anyone. Look at your Grandma. She ain't cried yet. It ain't natural. You oughtta be thinking of her. Dry your tears now and try to help your Grandma cry."

I looked. Grandma was erect and dry-eyed in her wheelchair. There was not a trace of expression on her face, not even when she looked straight at me.

"Grandma, I love you."

She didn't respond. She wheeled her chair to the grave, picked up a handful of dirt and dropped it into the opening. She took the corsage from her dress and dropped it in, too. She turned and wheeled her way back to the funeral car.

"Come on, Jack. Let's go home."

I got in slowly, reluctantly.

Later that night, I was sitting in Grandma's room with her. All of a sudden, she had a strange look on her face.

"Are you ok Grandma?" I asked.

"Can you see him Jack?" Grandma asked me.

"See who?" I looked around the room. There was no one there.

"Uncle Carroll."

"I don't see him."

"I do. He's right next to you. Hello, son."

I looked again and saw nothing. Grandma's face was set in a strange smile.

"I understand, son," she said. "Can I touch you? Can you touch me? Oh, son. Oh, Carroll. I love you. Can't you stay a little longer? Goodbye, son. Thank you. Thank you, dear Jesus. Come here, Jackie."

I sat on the footrest of her wheelchair and laid my head in her lap. "What'd you see, Grandma?"

"I saw your Uncle Carroll."

A chill went down my spine as I accepted that she really had seen him. "What'd he say?"

"Oh, Jack, it was so beautiful. I couldn't tell who it was, at first. I thought it might be my own beloved mother. The light was blue and shimmery, like a living fog. Then his face became clear and the upper part of his body. Then he spoke to me"

"Don't worry, Mother. The important part of me is here."

"Then I saw that he had no legs. I asked about touchin'. He just smiled and shook his head no. All of a sudden, Jackie, my worries and fears were gone. They were taken away. I feel more peaceful than I ever remember feelin'. Jackie, go to bed now. I want to cry." I went to the kitchen and stood behind the door. I listened to her cry for a long time. I cried myself as I heard her give prayers of thanks and gratitude. She was still praying when I went to bed and fell into a profound sleep.

BAILEY

When I got home from school, Grandma was waiting at the front door for me.

"Jackie, I'm glad you came straight home. Something's wrong with Spot."

Spot was a white rat terrier with a black saddle. He was Grandma's dog and no one else's. He'd sit in her lap for hours at a time but wouldn't let anyone else touch him.

"What's wrong?"

"I think he must have a cockroach caught in his throat. I went to the bathroom this afternoon and Spot, just like he always does, went ahead and chased the cockroaches away. Only, this time, I'm afraid he swallowed one. He's been coughin' and gaggin' ever since. I tried to look down his throat but he wouldn't let me. You got any idea what we can do?"

"Call a vet, I guess. I dunno."

"Vets cost money and you know we ain't got none to spare on a dog."

"Billy told me once that Doc Bailey comes to see poor people's pets and sometimes doesn't even charge."

"It's worth a try. Poor dog. Would you go next door and see if you can use their phone to call him?"

"They're mad at me."

"What on earth for?"

"'Cause I shot some sparrows with my BB gun and they died in their yard."

"Oh, Jackie."

"They was mad when they told me but I was glad. I was thinkin' I missed 'em."

"Go anyway. Tell 'em I told you to."

"Ok, but don't be surprised…"

"Just shut up and go."

"Ok, ok."

Doc Bailey came by about seven that night. Supper was over and the dishes washed and put away. Spot, used to getting tidbits at the table, ate nothing but continued to cough and gag. Grandma was a nervous wreck out of frustration and helplessness. When Doc knocked at the door, she finally settled down.

"Thank Jesus," she said. "Jackie, you let him in."

"Hi son! I'm Doc Bailey. You got a sick dog here?" His voice came from deep in his chest and sort of rolled out like big rocks. He was short and squat but looked very powerful. His face was short and squat too, more like a square than an oblong. Beneath his wavy, silver hair, his forehead, eye corners, and cheeks were full of deep lines. His mouth looked like he was smiling, even when he wasn't.

Grandma had Spot up on the kitchen table which she'd covered with newspaper. She held him there with one hand on his chest, the other on his back. No sooner than Doc reached for him than Spot bit him right on the web between the thumb and first finger. It bled immediately. Grandma kept a fly swatter hanging on the side of her wheelchair arm. I grabbed it and went to hit Spot with it.

"Bad dog!" I yelled.

Doc caught my arm in mid-air. His huge hand curled around my wrist and I couldn't move it any which way. "We never, never, never hit a sick animal," he said.

"Ok," I whined. "I wasn't gonna hit him hard. You're bleedin' on me. Let go."

He let me twist away and I put the swatter back on its hook. I went over and sat down on the far side of the room. He tried twice more to lay hands on Spot but couldn't.

"Hey!" he said. "I can handle bulls and horses but this little feller's got me stumped. Come over here, son," he said to me. "You'll have to control him while I check him out."

Spot wanted to bite my fingers off, too.

"Grab him by the scruff of his neck with your right hand. Now run your left hand over his muzzle from the back, then clamp it shut. A dog has powerful muscles for closing his jaws, but very weak ones for opening them."

"Like this?" I asked.

"Good boy! You did it perfect the very first time. How old are you?"

Right away I liked this man. I couldn't remember anyone ever saying "good boy" before. Instead, I was always being put down for not doing something better, or sooner, or not at all. It was amazing how proud those two words made me feel.

"Almost sixteen."

"You got a job?"

"No, sir. I had one at a drugstore but the owner didn't like me so I quit."

"Well, I like you just fine," he said as he greased a thermometer and stuck it up Spot's rectum. "You think you'd like to work for me?"I dunno."

"Well," he said, "it's easy to see you have a natural way with dogs. My other boy quit a couple of weeks ago. He joined the army. You could use the money, couldn't you?"

"What would I have to do?"

"Clean the cages, feed and water the animals, give them their medications, and assist me with my examinations and treatments."

"Could I learn anything?"

"You could learn as much as you wanted to learn. I'll be glad to teach you. I'll pay you ten dollars a week plus carfare. We got a deal?" Doc slipped the thermometer out. "Hmm, one-hundred-and-four, just a little high for a dog. You hold his neck and front paws. I want to look down his throat. Has he been eating anything unusual?"

"Just cockroaches," said Grandma. "He don't actually eat 'em; he just kills 'em."

"Well, he's got a leg caught in his throat. I can see it in there now." He took a pair of forceps and pulled the leg out. "A cockroach leg is filled with tiny barbs. He's gonna be all right. You got any aspirin?"

"Yes, doctor."

"Give him half of one tonight and a half of one three times tomorrow. I'll stop by tomorrow night. Whatta you say, son? Want to come to work for me?"

"I think you should, Jackie," said Grandma.

"Ok, sure, I guess so. Why not?"

"Good. Good. I'll expect you tomorrow right after school." He gave me directions to the hospital, then said, "You want to learn how to give a pill? Get me the aspirin bottle." I did. Doc broke one in half. "Put your palm over his eyes. Now squeeze his lips in against his back teeth until he opens his mouth. Now tilt his head back, drop the pill into the back of his throat and push it way down with two fingers. Now close his mouth and stroke his throat until you're sure he's swallowed it. Beautiful. I couldn't have done it better myself. You're a bright lad."

I felt myself blush. "I think I'm gonna like workin' with dogs," I said.

"Not just dogs. I work with cats, sheep, cattle, horses, pigs, and sometimes monkeys and birds."

"Gee! Do I get to, too?"

"You sure do. See you tomorrow?"

"Yes, sir!"

Doc left and Grandma beamed. "Good for you, Jack! I was worried when you quit your other job but I see now it was needless. The Good Lord just wanted you to have a better job, that's all. Be sure to thank Him when you say your prayers tonight."

"I will, Grandma." And I did.

PAIN

The couple, in their fifties and dressed upper middle class, brought their cocker spaniel in, wrapped in a blanket. It was seven at night. I'd just finished cleaning up after three spaying operations. The operating/examination room was to the left as you entered the hospital. There was a four by eight glass window in the wall separating it from the combined office/waiting room on the right. The people didn't wait to be asked but brought their dog straight in and laid it on the stainless steel, two foot by six foot table. The woman was crying and the man looked grim.

"What do we have here?" asked Doc with a grin in his voice.

"You'd better look for yourself," said the man.

"All right." Doc peeled back the blanket, shook his head and frowned. There was no grin in his voice as he asked, "How the hell did this happen?"

"We went on vacation," said the man in an unsteady voice. "We left plenty of food and water running in the pan. We just got back and found him this way."

"Look at this, son," said Doc. "This dog had a wound, might have been just a scratch. Flies got to it, laid their eggs and look what happened." He pulled the belly skin away with a pair of forceps. The area between the skin and the meat was white with crawling maggots. "They go a lot further than what you can see. This dog's been literally skinned alive." He turned to face the owners. He looked stern. "Do you want me to put him to sleep?"

The woman cried harder. The man, clenching his jaw and speaking through his teeth said, "No. If there's a chance in hell, we want him saved. We have a lot of make up to him."

"You sure as hell do," said Doc. "Son, get me that gallon of chloroform from the storeroom."

It suffered in silence as Doc submerged its body in chloroform. When I complained about the suffering the animal did, as shown by its weak, soft crying, Doc said, "Jack, a doctor sometimes has to create pain in order to save a life. What I did is nothing. Your real complaint ought to be against the people who put their pets in harm's way. This dog will be back at its masters' feet, wagging its tail and totally ignorant of how it was hurt. That's the sad part." He said it right in front of the owners. They had no reply. The woman cried a little harder; the man looked a little grimmer."Tell you what, son, I've got two farm calls to make Sunday. How'd you like to come along? It might teach you more about the good uses of pain."

"What's gonna happen?"

"We're going to vaccinate a horse and cure a case of warts in a young bull. Want to come?"

"Sure."

"Good boy."

Doc picked me up at eight AM. "Hope you don't mind getting out this early. I want to get done and relax this afternoon."

"I don't mind. It's a beautiful morning."

"What am I gonna learn about pain?"

"How it's used to control large animals. There's no way you can match their strength, so you control them through pain. Don't ask any more questions about it. You'll learn soon enough."

We were quiet the rest of the way out to the farm. It was a good looking farm. Everything was clean and orderly right down to the firewood stacked in neat rows beside the well-maintained white farmhouse. The farmer was neat and clean, too. He was big and so was the horse. He had a bridle on the horse and had him confined to a corral that was the front yard of two closely spaced barns. He met us at the corral gate.

"Hi Doc!" He shook hands.

"Hi Henry. This is my assistant, Jack. He's going to learn about a twitch."

He shook hands with me too. His hand was huge and strong, but he didn't clamp down hard, just firm. "First timer, huh?" said the farmer. "Well, we all gotta start somewhere. You want my twitch or you got your own?"

"We'll use yours," said Doc.

The farmer went into one of the barns and brought out an ax handle. Instead of a steel blade, it had a short loop of rope at its end. He handed it to me.

"Whatta I do with it?"

"You slip the loop over his nose and twist it tight, good and tight, so he won't move when he feels the needle," said Doc.

Henry held the horse by the bridle. I walked up, slipped the noose over its nose and twisted what I thought was hard enough. The horse reared, snatching the ax handle right out of my hands. I disappeared in the opening between the two barns. Henry and Doc were laughing fit to split a gut.

"Come on out, Jack," laughed Doc. "The first time's free."

"I can't. I'm stuck."

Doc and Henry laughed again. Henry grabbed my arm near the shoulder and yanked me free.

"Come on, son," said Doc. "This time, twist that twitch as hard as you can, then give it an extra turn. The whole idea is to cause so much pain, he won't move."

I twisted the twitch until I thought the animal's nose would come off. Doc finished the injection and the horse, except for trembling, stood stock still.

"Alright, you can let go now."

I undid the twitch and backed off swiftly, fearful that the horse might want revenge. Henry and Doc laughed again.

"Come on, boy. We got a Black Angus bull waiting for us."

The next farm was more cluttered and littered. The barn needed painting and the firewood was all in one big pile. The place didn't look uncared for, just half-cared for.

The farmer met us at a corral fenced with three-inch iron pipe. He didn't offer to shake hands. The corral covered an area about the size of a house with weeds and cow pies on the ground. In it was a single Black Angus bull, about three-quarters grown.

"Doc, this bull was pasture bred and raised. He's a little wild, so be careful."

Doc stood with one foot resting on the bottom rail, his arms over the top rail and looked at the animal. It had several clusters of warts from tea-cup size to hat size.

"Those warts sure do look ugly. They don't harm the bull at all but they sure do look ugly. They're caused by a virus, son. One shot of vaccine will knock them right out. You think you can rope him and get him up to the fence?"

"Sure, I can," I said, believing with the belief of ignorance.

"Well, go ahead then."

I felt like Tom Mix, Gene Autry, and Roy Rogers all rolled into one as I ducked under and strode into the center of the corral, lasso in hand. I twirled the noose around my head and threw. It missed. Doc and the farmer were grinning. I blushed and tried again and again and again. They were laughing out loud now.

"Try walkin' up to him and drop the noose over his head," said the farmer.

I approached the bull slowly, cooing as I went. "Hey, bully, bully. Easy now. Easy." I got close enough to drop the noose over the bull's head. The bull just stood there until the noose was tightened, then it took off. I tried to hold onto the rope. It burned blisters across both palms. Adrenaline stopped the pain, however, and the bull stopped near the fence where the other two waited. I again approached gently and looped the rope over the top rail. Then I slowly tightened it until the bull was right up to the fence. Doc handed me what appeared to be a pair of pliers. Instead of jaws, however, they had blunt knobs on the end.

"This is a bull leader," he said. "You stick them in the bull's nose and clamp down hard, just like you did with the twitch."

I tied the rope to the rail, took the bull leader and tried to stick it in the bull's nose. I was too slow in clamping down. As soon as the bull felt the cold metal, he reared, breaking the knot and flailing the air with his front hooves. One hoof caught me right in the mouth. My brain sped up so fast that everything seemed to be in slow motion. I looked down to see my two front teeth floating to the ground like feathers.

"God damn, I lost my teeth," was all I said. Doc and the farmer rushed to me. I grinned at them through the gap in my upper teeth. "I'm all right," I said. "I hated them damn buck teeth anyway."

"I've got to get him back," said Doc to the farmer. "When the shock wears off, he'll be in a lot of pain. I've got some codeine at the office."

"Sure, Doc. Sorry this had to happen."

"You get that bull cross-tied in a stanchion and I'll be by next Sunday."

"Ok, Doc. Sorry kid."

By the time we got back, the pain had set in. I was very glad for the codeine.

GRADUATION

Graduation was just around the corner and I was scared stiff. I'd have to get a job and had no idea of what I wanted to do. I knew I didn't want to work in the feed mills or stockyards. I knew I didn't want to accept Doc Bailey's generous offer. He'd made it a week ago and had been cool to me ever since because I turned him down.

"Son," he said, "you took to this work like you were born to it. I've given you every responsibility and you haven't let me down yet. How'd you like to be a vet?"

"I wouldn't."

He was instantly angry but I could see him controlling it.

"Well, why the hell not? I'm telling you, I'd pay your way through vet school and turn over my practice to you a couple of years after graduation. I'm tired of being tired, son. I want to be retired. You're always talking about wanting an education. Well, here's your chance."

"I just can't, Doc."

He didn't say anything. He just went to his gin bottle and had a bigger swig than usual. Then he came back. "Jack, what makes you so different?"

"I ain't different."

"Sure you are. I've never had a boy like you. I teach you about fractures and the next thing I know, you're diagnosing a compound comminuted fracture. And rightly too. You've diagnosed meningitis, strychnine poisoning, distemper and a dozen other diseases. And you're always right. You're quite a bright boy, you know."

"Naw, I ain't. Leastwise, that's what everybody says. They're always callin' me a smarty-pants and Mr. Know-It-All. I just learned to keep my mouth shut and ears and eyes open just like my daddy told me to. No one else thinks I'm smart. Every time I tell someone what I know, I get in trouble.

"One time I had this friend called Carl Messner. He had to stay inside one day so I went to keep him company through the screen door. I started tellin' him how babies was made. His big brother was listenin' in and came and made me shut up and go away. He never let Carl play with me again.

"I got even, though. He was the assistant scout master and always carried this .22 automatic when we went to camp. Slept with it under his pillow. One night, me and some guys stole this pickled snake from the nature room and coiled it up on his chest while he was asleep on his back. Then we made noise to wake him up. "Well, he grabbed his gun and shot seven times as fast as he could pull the trigger. He shot the snake to smithereens and even nicked his big toe. Everyone else was afraid but I just stood there and laughed. They made him quit taking his gun. Then they made me quit the scouts. Said I was incorrigible. Everyone else had blamed the whole thing on me. I didn't care, though. I already knew most of the stuff they was tryin' to teach us."

Doc listened to the whole story without interrupting once. He smiled when I was done. "That just proves what I've been trying to tell you. You know an awful lot for someone so young. Why don't you want to go to vet school?"

I decided to level with him. "How long is vet school, Doc?"

"I think its five years now."

"Five years! I thought it was only four! I can't wait five years to start earnin' some money! Besides that, I'm sick of seein' death and sufferin' all the time. Too many animals go out the back door for the rubbish man."

"If they weren't going out the back door, son, they wouldn't be coming in the front. It's no different than any other business. You can't make a hundred percent in anything."

"I guess I know that's true, but I hate it. Watchin' a dog or cat die makes me furious. I can't see why God makes anything suffer so much. Why can't He just take 'em?"

"I don't know Jack. Can't you focus on the ones that do make it?"

"Not really. They have to go through a lot of pain too. It ain't fair. You know what I think? I think God really doesn't care. I'll tell you somethin'. I used to pray for these animals when I first started here. Finally, I quit because it didn't do no good at all. I'm sick of it. Once I leave here, I don't ever want to see it again. Sorry, Doc, but that's the way I feel."

"Well, think about it, son."

"Ain't no use to. My mind's made up."

Doc shook his head, clapped me on the back, and headed for the back room for another guzzle of gin.

GRANDPA

The day's classes were over; hard, tough classes where the instructors expected you to retain everything they said. Since half of what they said was in Russian, few students succeeded. Already, after just twelve weeks of a forty-eight week course, over half of my class had dropped out. I was determined not to be one of their number. This was what I'd joined the service for—a higher education. This was my chance to make, if not good, at least better than any of my family had done before. If I learned this difficult Russian language, prestige would be mine, and self-esteem. Respect and honor would replace the shame and sorrow that was my family legacy.

There were several hours of homework ahead of me. With a buddy, I was studying the declension of irregular Russian verbs, memorizing a one-hundred-fifty line vocabulary of technical terms, and restudying the lessons of yesterday where I had been less than perfect. Home was a cot, wall locker, and foot locker on the second floor of a barracks housing fifty-nine other men. I had just reached my peak level of concentration when a sergeant interrupted me.

"You have an emergency phone call in the orderly room."

I knew it was Grandma. I'd had one of these in basic training. I got an emergency leave. Grandpa was in the hospital, it was winter, and she had no one to carry in the coal, carry out the ashes, chop kindling wood, and shovel snow.

"Excuse me, Dick," I said to my buddy, "I won't be long."

The orderly room was just up the hill from the barracks. The night was foggy. The smell from the cannery on the shore of Monterey, California filled the fog with a stench that penetrated everything in the Presidio. I hurried along.

"Hello?"

"Jack, this is Grandma. Grandpa died this morning."

I closed my eyes. Images of him flashed through my mind like mist being chased across a lake by the rising sun. Sitting on his lap, learning to read the funny papers. He never got impatient. He made everything fun no matter how slow I was. He would laugh when I got something right and cheer me on when I got something wrong. He made me love words and their music. God, how I loved that man.

Sitting at the round oak table with the claw legs, learning to play rummy and solitaire. Listening to how he helped lynch a black man, beating him first with bull whips, then tying him to the roof of the school where he'd raped a white woman, then setting the building on fire. Why did I love him so much?I was working in the backyard garden when I heard Grandma and Grandpa fighting. It wasn't a normal fight. Both were shouting curses at each other, words I didn't know Grandma even knew. When I heard Grandma yell, "Go ahead and kill me, you son-of-a-bitch!" I rushed into the house. Grandma sat slumped in her wheelchair, her legs straight out, her arms out to the sides, her head thrown back. Grandpa had a butcher knife against her throat. When I burst through the door, Grandpa looked up, hesitated, threw the knife into the sink and ran out the front door. He was gone for twelve days.

Grandpa, you, in your own way, were just as cruel as Grandma. My love for her had slowly faded away. Did my love for you die too?

How come I love this old man? He never whipped me and he never lied to me. Is that enough? He's mean to Grandma, always trying to embarrass her with his cussing and always putting her down and giving her orders. He's one man to me and another one to her. How come I love him? Is it because that's what I'm supposed to do? He's a killer and a lynch mobber, and more. Why should I love him?

I was home from basic training with a PFC stripe and a crew cut.

"Come on, Jack! I wanna buy you a beer and show you off to my friends. You don't mind if I brag a little on you, do you?"

"Sure, Grandpa."

The bar was empty except for the barmaid and one drunk sitting at the bar.

"Sally, this is my grandson, Jack. He just got back from boot camp. He's goin' to spy school to learn Roosian. Give us a beer."

We sat next to the drunk, Grandpa between me and him. The drunk started cursing. Grandpa took offense. "Where I come from, we don't use language like that in front of womenfolk."

"You wanna make me shut up?"

He and Grandpa slid off their stools at the same time. Grandpa hit him once with an uppercut from off the floor and laid him flat on his back. The drunk reached in his pocket and drew out a knife. Grandpa stomped it out of his hand and was trying to stomp his face when I reached him and pulled him back.

"Son-of-a-bitch, I believe I broke my thumb. Come on, let's have our beer."

He slid back on his stool and lifted his full glass with his left hand. There wasn't a tremor. The man on the floor got up, went to the men's room and left out the front door without a word. Grandpa never gave him another look. I wished I was that brave. Eighty-one years old and doesn't even know it. Bad seed. I must be bad, too, bad enough to be deserted by my own dad. Could I be cruel, too?

"Jack, are you still there?"

"Yeah, Grandma, I'm here."

"Are you comin' back for the funeral?"

"No, I ain't."

"Why not?"

"Grandpa wouldn't want me to. If I left now, I'd wash out. I could never catch up. Russian is hard, harder even than college, some say. You don't want me to miss out on this chance, do you? I know Grandpa wouldn't."

"No, Jack, not really."

"Besides, the only thing Dad ever taught me that's any good was not to quit, to never ever quit. I ain't. I'm not comin' back."

She paused for a long time. "Will I ever see you again?"

"Sure, Grandma. Sure you will."